MAKING MUSIC YOUR OWN

BEATRICE LANDECK
Writer and Lecturer

ELIZABETH CROOK
Associate Professor of Music
University of Delaware

HAROLD C. YOUNGBERG
Director of Music Education
Oakland Public Schools, California

special consultant for basic music concepts
OTTO LUENING
Composer
Professor of Music
Columbia University, New York

special contributors

SAMUEL BARBER *5th grade*

CARLOS CHÁVEZ *5th grade*

AARON COPLAND *4th grade*

HENRY COWELL *3rd and 4th grades*

PAUL CRESTON *6th grade*

NORMAN DELLO JOIO *4th grade*

OTTO LUENING *6th grade*

RICHARD RODGERS *6th grade*

WILLIAM SCHUMAN *5th grade*

IGOR STRAVINSKY *6th grade*

illustrated by
DAVID KLEIN

Silver Burdett Company MORRISTOWN, NEW JERSEY
A Division of General Learning Corporation

MAKING MUSIC YOUR OWN

PARK RIDGE, ILL. • PALO ALTO • DALLAS • ATLANTA

Acknowledgments

The authors and editors of MAKING MUSIC YOUR OWN acknowledge with gratitude the contributions, aid, and advice of the following persons and organizations:

THE ADVISORY BOARD

Neva Aubin, Oakland, Calif....Imogene Hilyard, Columbus, Ohio...Mary Jaye, South Orange, N. J....Carl Licht, Mount Vernon, N.Y....Mary Val Marsh, San Diego, Calif. ...Lucille Mitchell, Arlington, Va....Marguerite O'Day, Denver, Colo. . . . David Wilmot, Gainesville, Fla. . . . A. Verne Wilson, Portland, Ore.

SPECIAL CONTRIBUTORS

Pura Belpré, Latin-American folk tales . . . Edith Fowke, Canadian folk songs . . . Ruth Tooze, Children's literature.

CONSULTANTS

Oneyda Alvarenga, Curator of Folklore Archives, São Paulo, Brazil...Adelina Ardittis, Contributor of Greek folk songs...Isabel Aretz, Field collector of South American folklore, author, musicologist...Louise Borg, Contributor of Oriental folk songs . . . Atsuko Fennema, Professional singer of Japanese folk songs . . . June Honda, Elementary teacher from Japan...Leo LeBlanc, Collector of Acadian folk songs . . . Adeeb Madanat, Elementary teacher from Jordan...Fernando Ortiz, Field collector of Afro-Cuban folklore, author, musicologist...David Polutnik, Professor of Russian language...Andrés Sas, Authority on Peruvian folk songs . . . Carleton Sprague Smith, Musicologist...J. Laurence Willhide, Musicologist.

RESOURCE ORGANIZATIONS

African Music Society; Hugh Tracey, Secy. . . . Greater New York Council for Foreign Students, Inc. . . . International Folk Music Council; Maud Karpeles, Secy.

Credit and appreciation are due publishers and copyright owners for use of the following:

"African Proverbs" from AFRICAN PROVERBS compiled by Charlotte and Wolf Leslau, copyright 1962, The Peter Pauper Press.

"Alekoki" dance directions from GROWTH THROUGH PHYSICAL EDUCATION by A. K. Chang, published by the Department of Education, Honolulu, Hawaii.

"Earth and Sky" from POEMS FOR CHILDREN, copyright 1927, renewed 1955, Eleanor Farjeon. Reprinted by permission of J. B. Lippincott, publishers, and Harold Ober Associates Incorporated.

"For the Beauty of the Earth" from the estate of F. S. Pierpoint, by permission of Oxford University Press.

"French" from POEMS FOR CHILDREN, copyright 1938, Eleanor Farjeon. Reprinted by permission of J. B. Lippincott, publishers, and Harold Ober Associates Incorporated.

"Hallowe'en Indignation Meeting" from POEMS MADE UP TO TAKE OUT, © 1963, Margaret Fishback. Published by David McKay Company, Inc.

"Hello, Pretty Girls" collected by Professor Andrés Sas, Lima, Peru.

"Mark you there yonder" from BEYOND THE HIGH HILLS — A Book of Eskimo Poems, collected by Knud Rasmussen, copyright © 1961, The World Publishing Company.

"The Ninepenny Fidel" words by permission of S. D. Campbell.

"Other Children" by permission of Helen Wing.

"The Returning Hunter" from the Sixth Annual Report of the Bureau of American Ethnology, Washington, D. C.

"The Sea Wolf" © 1923, The New York Times Company. Reprinted by permission.

"Something Told the Wild Geese" reprinted with permission of the publisher from BRANCHES GREEN by Rachel Field. Copyright 1934, The Macmillan Company, renewed 1962, Arthur S. Pederson.

Music Autographs: MAXWELL WEANER • Cover: THOMAS VROMAN • Designer: E. JOAN STEPHANI

Photo Credits: HENRY GROSKINSKY, pp. 19, 47, 61; NEW YORK TIMES, p. 28 (bottom); FRED FEHL, pp. 28-29; COLUMBIA RECORDS, pp. 110-111; MARK KAUFFMAN, pp. 128-129; ALFRED EISENSTAEDT, pp. 168-169

Contents

The earth is the Lord's, and the fulness
thereof; the world, and they that dwell therein.

For the Beauty of the Earth

Folliott S. Pierpoint   Conrad Kocher

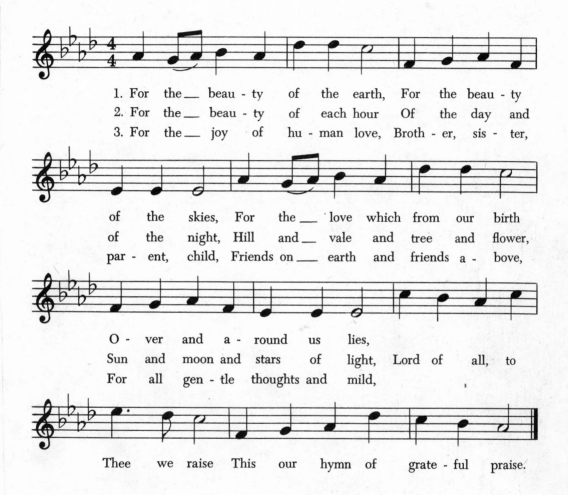

1. For the __ beau-ty of the earth, For the beau-ty
2. For the __ beau-ty of each hour Of the day and
3. For the __ joy of hu-man love, Broth-er, sis-ter,

of the skies, For the __ love which from our birth
of the night, Hill and __ vale and tree and flower,
par-ent, child, Friends on __ earth and friends a-bove,

O-ver and a-round us lies,
Sun and moon and stars of light, Lord of all, to
For all gen-tle thoughts and mild,

Thee we raise This our hymn of grate-ful praise.

Give Me a Song to Sing

English Words by Ruth Martin   Italian Folk Song

I don't wish for lots of mon - ey, Or for fame that nev - er ends.

All I want is bread and hon - ey And some good and faith - ful friends.

Oh, give me a song to sing, Oh, give me a song to sing,

Oh, give me a song to sing, And I'll be hap - py as a king.

Rarakatom!

English Words by Ruth Martin   Hungarian Folk Song

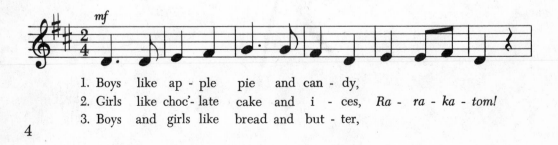

1. Boys like ap - ple pie and can - dy,
2. Girls like choc'- late cake and i - ces, *Ra - ra - ka - tom!*
3. Boys and girls like bread and but - ter,

4

Boys   like ap - ple   pie   and can - dy,
Girls   like choc'- late   cake   and i - ces, *Ra - ra - ka - tom!*
Boys   and girls like   bread   and but - ter,

f **Refrain**

Though   all   boys   like   pie   and   can - dy,
Though   all   girls   like   cake   and   i - ces,
Though   they   all   like   bread   and   but - ter,

p

They   think   sing - ing   songs   is   dan - dy.
Still   they   think   that   danc - ing's   nic - est.
They   like   best   to   meet   each   oth - er.

f   *p*

Ra - ra - ka - ti - rom,   ra - ra - ka - ti - rom,

f   *p*

Ra - ra - ka - tom!   Ra - ra - ka - tom!

This song is in two sections — the verse (A) and the refrain (B). There is an echo part in section B. As you listen, follow the notation and join in on the echo part.

Section A is made up of two phrases. Listen to hear how they are alike. Can you hear how the two phrases are different?

When a tonal pattern or a short melody is repeated starting on a different pitch, the repetition is called a **sequence**. As you sing the song again, notice when you are singing a sequence and when you are singing an echo part.

The German Band

English Words by Margaret Marks   German Folk Song

Village bands are popular in Germany. Sometimes they are marching bands with brass and percussion instruments. The instruments are played by citizens of the town — firemen, policemen, and merchants.

Play as an introduction and continue throughout:

Come and hear the Ger - man band, Ger - man band, Ger - man band!

Oh, the weath - er is so grand for the big pa - rade!

6

Verse

1. First there comes the drum - mer, And as a drum - mer,
2. Next come brass - es play - ing, It sounds like neigh - ing
3. Next comes our po - lice force, Three men and one horse,

He's quite a plumb - er! He's off the beat in ev - 'ry
Or don - keys bray - ing! And all the peo - ple there are
I won - der who's boss! Al - though their lead - er shouts his

D. C. al Fine

num - ber, And no one knows how come They let him drum._
say - ing, "Let's stuff 'em up with hay So they won't play!"_
head off, With his *a - hep, a - hep,* They're out of step! _

Look at the notation of
the drum part:

$\frac{2}{4}$ ♩ ♩ | ♩ ♩ | ♩ ♩ | ♩ ♩ |

In the illustration above, you see beats that are pictured in
quarter notes. These are measured off into groups of two by a
bar line. In this song, the two beats picture the "left — right"
of marching feet. Chant "left — right" as you look at the notes
above. How many times will you say "left — right"?

Which word is accented more than the other?

Did you notice that the accent is on the first note in each
measure? The first beat in the measure is the strong beat, or
the **downbeat.** A bar line is always placed *before* the downbeat.

The Rattlin' Bog

Irish Folk Song

Do you know how to sing a cumulative song?

Oh, row, the rat-tlin' bog, The bog down in the val-ley, oh,

Oh, row, the rat-tlin' bog, The bog down in the val-ley, oh.

1. And in that bog there was a tree,
2. And on that tree there was a bough,

A rare
tree,
bough, and a rat-tlin'
tree,
bough,

(1.) And the tree in the bog, And the tree in the bog,
(2.) And the bough on the tree, And the tree in the bog,

And the bog down in the val-ley, oh.

3. Now on that bough there was a branch,
   A rare branch, and a rattlin' branch,
   And the branch on the bough,
   And the bough on the tree,
   And the tree in the bog,
   And the bog down in the valley, oh.

4. Now on that branch there was a nest,
   A rare nest, and a rattlin' nest,
   And the nest on the branch,
   And the branch on the bough,
   And the bough on the tree,
   And the tree in the bog,
   And the bog down in the valley, oh.

5. Now in that nest there was a bird,
   A rare bird, and a rattlin' bird,
   And the bird in the nest,
   And the nest on the branch . . .

6. And on that bird there was a tail . . .

FINDING YOUR PLACE ON A KEYBOARD

The black keys will help you find your place on the keyboard. A group of two black keys is followed by a group of three black keys from one end of the keyboard to the other.

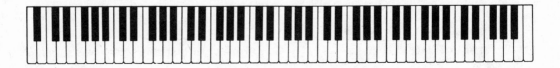

The arrangement of bars on the upper row of the tuned bells is the same as that of the black keys on the piano.

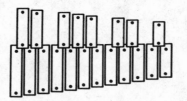

Play the first bar in a group of two on the upper row.

Find the first of another group of two. Now play the bells one after the other. Sing as you play.

The distance between the two tones is called an **octave**. Find another octave on the upper row.

Using the upper row as a guide, find and play octaves on the lower row. Start with low C and its octave. Sing as you play.

Feel how far apart the tones are as you sing an octave. Feel how far apart the bells are as you play an octave.

See how far the notes of the **octave** are from each other when they are written on the staff.

Using the upper row as a guide, see how fast you can play octaves. Can you find the octave in "The Rattlin' Bog"?

Look at the picture of the tuned bells to find another interval.

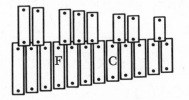

Notice the F bar to the left of the group of three bars on the upper row. Now notice the C bar above, which is to the left of the group of two bars on the upper row.

Call F "one" and count up, by steps on the lower row, to C (five). This distance, or interval, is called a **fifth**.

Play a fifth, starting on F. Play a fifth, starting on G. Use the upper row as a guide. Sing as you play.

Feel how far apart the tones are as you sing a fifth. Feel how far apart the bells are as you play a fifth. See how far the notes of the fifth are from each other when they are written on the staff.

F to C   G to D   E to A

Hand Me Down

Spiritual

Gabriel's silver trumpet was the inspiration for the words of this song. The song leader called out his solo to start the singing. The other voices responded in chorus.

Oh, hand me down, Hand me down,

Hand me down my sil - ver trum - pet, Ga - briel.

Hand me down, throw it down, An - y way to get it down,

Hand me down my sil - ver trum - pet, Lord. Oh, Lord.

Mo - ses had a lot to do, ____

Hand me down my sil - ver trum - pet, Ga - briel,

From GIT ON BOARD by Beatrice Landeck, ©1944, Edward B. Marks Music Corporation.

When he led the chil - dren of Is - ra - el through,

Hand me down my sil - ver trum - pet, Lord.

When you know the melody, study the notation to see where the chorus sings in two parts. The upper part starts on the fifth step of the scale. Where does the lower part start? The parts move to the tonal center in opposite directions.

Come, Let's Dance

English Words by Alice Firgau   13th Century French Round

Follow the notes on the staff as you listen to this song. Let your eyes follow the rise and fall of each of the two phrases.

The tonal center is in the first space of the staff. On which step of the scale does each phrase start?

Study the notation to see how the two phrases are alike and how they are different.

Come, let's dance and sing a song to - geth - er.

Come, we'll laugh and have a jol - ly time.

The Journeyman's Song

English Words by Nancy Rushmore   German Folk Song

Long ago a worker who moved from one place to another to
earn his living was called a journeyman.

1. Now I'll bid fare - well to mas - ter and his wife,
2. Lis - ten, ev - 'ry - one, re - mem - ber what I said:
3. To my friends and — foes, to young and old a - like,

Good - by to all of you who lead a hap - py life.
"Man must eat ev - 'ry day un - less that man be dead."
This I'll say a - gain: "On new paths I must hike!"

But be - fore I go, the — truth I'll tell,

work I do
The — meals you served nev - er pleased — me — well.
lo - cal girls

I will my luck be prov - ing by mov - ing.

As you listen to this song, can you discover how many phrases
there are? Can you hear which ones are alike?

14

On another day, take turns playing each of the patterns below on a percussion instrument.

Strong beat

Steady beat

Rhythm of the melody

A half note (𝅗𝅥) can take the place of two quarter notes (♩ ♩).

A quarter note (♩) can take the place of two eighth notes (♪ ♪).

REVIEW OF METER

Each pattern below is the notation for part of a familiar song. Study the patterns. Which question will you answer?

1. Can you match one of the patterns with "The Journeyman's Song"?

2. Can you find the other pattern in a song at the beginning of your book?

3. Can you play one of the patterns on an instrument and name the song from its rhythm?

4. Can you make up a rhythm pattern of your own, using ♩, 𝅗𝅥, and ♪♪ in ¾ or ⁴⁄₄ meter?

5. Can you tell by listening to a composition whether it moves in twos or threes?

SQUARE DANCE

Practice "calling" for this square dance. Say the words in the rhythm of the music. As you say them, think of the floor pattern the dancers will make in response to the call. All square dances start in this formation:

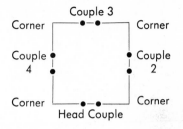

Introduction
Bow to your partners, bow to your corner.

Now you circle left, take a ride on a wheel,
Let yourself go from the head to the heel.
All the way round and don't be late,
You'll swing when you're home on your own front gate.

Swing her up and swing her down,
Swing her all the way to town.
Other way round, don't let her go.
Swing her on to Jericho.

1. Now join your hands and circle four,
   Go halfway round, not one step more.
   Then you duck for the oyster and dig for the clam,
   And you take a little dip in a frying pan.

2. Now on to the next and circle four,
   Go halfway round, not one step more.
   Then you duck for the oyster and dig for the clam,
   And you take a little dip in a jar of jam.

3. Now on to the next and circle four,
   Go halfway round, not one step more.
   Then you duck for the oyster and dig for the clam,
   And you take a little dip in the Boulder Dam.

4. You go round and round you go,
   Promenade all, each birdie and crow.
   Just keep on flying and don't be late
   Till you get back home to your own front gate.

17

LISTENING TO BRASS INSTRUMENTS

A brass instrument has a body of metal tubing, a mouthpiece at one end of the tube, and a bell-shaped opening at the other. To produce a tone, the player buzzes his lips into the mouthpiece and causes the air inside the tube to vibrate. The vibration travels through the length of the tube and becomes a tone. The bell helps to make the tone louder and helps to create the quality of the tone.

The player produces certain high and low tones on brass instruments by tightening or loosening his lips. Other tones are produced by changing the length of the column of air vibrating inside the instrument. Trumpet and horn players use three valves that open or close off sections of the tubing. A trombone player changes the tube length by moving the slide. Remember that the longer and larger the tube, the lower the pitch will be.

Look at the pictures of the trumpet, trombone, and French horn. Notice how the tubing is coiled in the trumpet and French horn. The tube of the trumpet is almost five feet long. It has fewer coils and bends than the French horn has. Because the tube is shorter, the trumpet produces higher tones than the horn.

The tube of the trombone is almost nine feet long, and the diameter of the tube is larger than that of either the horn or the trumpet. The trombone produces lower tones than the horn or trumpet.

For many years, composers have used the tempos, meters, and rhythms of certain popular dances in their compositions. They have given these pieces dance titles such as Gavotte and Minuet. People listen to this music rather than dance to it. A group of these pieces composed for listening can include fast, slow, lively, and graceful rhythms. A slow dance usually follows a fast dance. A dance in $\frac{2}{4}$ meter can follow one in $\frac{3}{4}$ or $\frac{6}{8}$ meter. A group of pieces that contrast in tempo, meter, and rhythm is called a **suite**.

Lyndol Mitchell has written a suite of three pieces called *Folk Suite*. In one of the pieces he gives his impression of a square dance as it would be danced by cowboys at a party called a hoedown. Listen to the following composition. Match the sounds of the brass instruments with their pictures.

Dance from Folk Suite .... Lyndol Mitchell

18

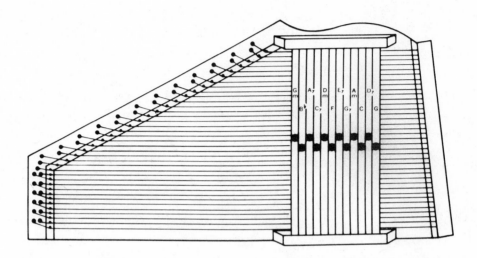

Place the autoharp in front of you so that you can read the letters on the bars. Find the F bar. Rest the index finger of the left hand on the button of the F bar. Now rest the middle finger of the left hand on the button of the C_7 bar. Notice that it is the next one in that row.

Seesaw back and forth by pressing one button after the other. Feel your way without looking. Strum the strings with your right hand.

When you press the F button and strum, you are sounding the F chord. When you press the C_7 button and strum, you are sounding the C_7 chord. Play one chord after the other several times to hear the difference in the sound of the two chords. Keep your fingertips resting on both buttons ready to press or release.

Now play the chords in rhythm, using the pattern shown here. Look at the notation, not at your fingers, as you strum.

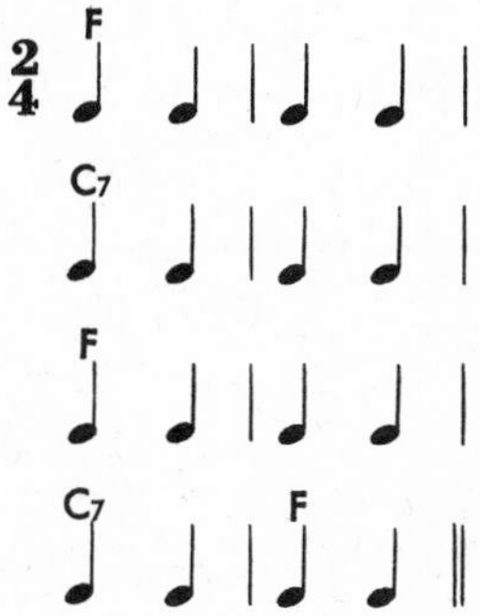

You can accompany "Skip to My Lou" and "Sandy Land" on the autoharp, using the pattern you have just played.

Skip to My Lou

Flies in the buttermilk, shoo, fly, shoo!
Flies in the buttermilk, shoo, fly, shoo!
Flies in the buttermilk, shoo, fly, shoo!
Skip to my Lou, my darling.

Sandy Land

Make my livin' in sandy land,
Make my livin' in sandy land,
Make my livin' in sandy land,
Ladies, fare you well.

Adapted from THE AMERICAN PLAY-PARTY SONG, with a Collection of Oklahoma Texts and Tunes, by B. A. Botkin, copyright 1937 by B. A. Botkin.

Find the G and D_7 buttons on the autoharp. Notice that the G and D_7 buttons are next to each other but on different rows. Play the G chord button with the index finger of the left hand and the D_7 button with the middle finger. Seesaw back and forth by pressing one button after the other. Look up as you play.

Accompany "Skip to My Lou" and "Sandy Land," using the G and D_7 chords. Use the F and C_7 pattern as a guide.

Look at the chord pattern for "Clementine." Practice the pattern to hear how the chords fit the melody. When you know how to change chords without looking at the notation or at your fingers, sing the song and play your own accompaniment.

Clementine

1. In a cavern by a canyon,
   Excavating for a mine,
   Dwelt a miner, forty-niner,
   And his daughter, Clementine.

Refrain
   Oh, my darling, oh, my darling,
   Oh, my darling Clementine,
   You are lost and gone forever,
   Dreadful sorry, Clementine.

2. Light she was and like a feather,
   And her shoes were number nine;
   Herring boxes without topses
   Sandals were for Clementine.

3. Drove she ducklings to the water
   Every morning just at nine;
   Struck her foot against a splinter,
   Fell into the foaming brine.

4. Rosy lips above the water
   Blowing bubbles mighty fine;
   But, alas! I was no swimmer,
   So I lost my Clementine.

Look at the chord pattern for "Polly Wolly Doodle."

Practice the chord pattern on the autoharp, then sing the song and play your own accompaniment.

Polly Wolly Doodle

1. Oh, I went down South for to see my Sal,
   Singing Polly Wolly Doodle all the day;
   My Sal, she is a spunky gal,
   Singing Polly Wolly Doodle all the day.

Refrain
   Fare thee well, fare thee well,
   Fare thee well my fairy fay,
   For I'm goin' to Louisiana, for to see my Susyanna,
   Singing Polly Wolly Doodle all the day.

2. Oh, my Sal, she is a maiden fair,
   Singing Polly Wolly Doodle all the day;
   With curly eyes and laughing hair,
   Singing Polly Wolly Doodle all the day.

3. The partridge is a pretty bird,
   It has a speckled breast,
   It steals away the farmer's grain,
   And totes it to its nest!

4. The raccoon's tail is ringed around,
   The 'possum's tail is bare,
   The rabbit's got no tail at all,
   Just a little bitty bunch of hair!

5. The June-bug he has golden wings,
   The lightning bug totes a flame,
   The caterpillar's got no wings at all,
   But he gets there just the same!

The bawl of a steer,
To a cowboy's ear,
  Is music of sweetest strain;
And the yelping notes
Of the gay coyotes
  To him are a glad refrain.

For a kingly crown
In the noisy town
  His saddle he wouldn't change;
No life so free
As the life we see
  Way out on the Yaso range.

The rapid beat
Of his broncho's feet
  On the sod as he speeds along,
Keeps living time
To the ringing rhyme
  Of his rollicking cowboy song.

The winds may blow
And the thunder growl
  Or the breezes may safely moan;—
A cowboy's life
Is a royal life,
  His saddle his kingly throne.

JOHN A. LOMAX

Git Along, Little Dogies

Cowboy Song

The cowpuncher sings a rollicking song as he prods the cattle along.

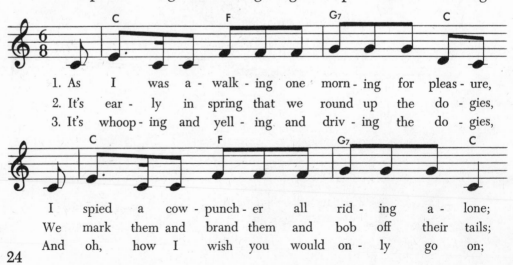

1. As I was a-walk-ing one morn-ing for pleas-ure,
2. It's ear-ly in spring that we round up the do-gies,
3. It's whoop-ing and yell-ing and driv-ing the do-gies,

I spied a cow-punch-er all rid-ing a-lone;
We mark them and brand them and bob off their tails;
And oh, how I wish you would on-ly go on;

His hat was throwed back and his spurs was a - jin - gling,
We round up our hors - es, load up the chuck wag - on,
It's whoop - ing and punch - ing, go on, lit - tle do - gies,

And as he ap - proach'd he was sing - ing this song:
And then throw the do - gies out on - to the trail.
You know that Wy - o - ming will be your new home.

Refrain

Whoop - ee ti - yi - yo, git a - long, lit - tle do - gies,

It's your mis - for - tune and none of my own;

Whoop- ee ti - yi - yo, git a - long lit - tle do - gies,

You know that Wy - o - ming will be your new home.

Think about life on the western plains and all the things a cowboy has to do on his job. Choose two cowboy activities to pantomime — one for the verse and the other for the refrain.

The rhythm of this song suggests the sound of horses' hoofs as they lope along. Play the rhythm on an instrument to accompany your dramatization.

The Goat

American Folk Song

Two groups can take part in singing this tall tale. One group will sing the melody. The other group, imitating the first, will sing in those places where the melody notes are held.

1. There was a man, (there was a man), now please take note, (now please, etc.),
2. One day that goat _____ felt frisk and fine, _____
3. But when the train _____ hove in - to sight _____

There was a man _____ who had a goat. _____
Ate three red shirts _____ from off the line. _____
That goat grew pale _____ and green with fright. _____

He loved that goat, _____ in - deed he did, _____
The man, he grabbed _____ him by the back _____
He heaved a sigh _____ as if in pain, _____

He loved that goat _____ just like a kid. _____
And tied him to _____ a rail - road track. _____
Coughed up those shirts _____ and flagged the train. _____

26

Great Granddad

American Cowboy Song

Cowboys like to talk about the old days in the West. In the evening, they gather around the campfire to sing and to tell tall tales. Sometimes they invite the girls to square dance.

1. Great Grand-dad, when the land was young,____
2. Twenty-one chil-dren____ came to bless The
3. Great Grand-dad was a bus-y man,____

Barred the door with a wag-on tongue,
old man's home in the wil-der-ness.
Cooked his grub in a fry-ing pan,

For the times was rough and the red-skins mocked,
They ____ slept on the floor with the dogs and cats,
He ____ picked his teeth with his hunt-ing knife,

And he said his prayers with his shot-gun cocked.
And they hunted in the woods in their coon-skin caps.
And he wore the same suit____ all his life.

Aaron Copland's music helps dancers bring the legend of Billy the Kid to life.

Aaron Copland, a busy composer, also spends much time conducting and teaching.

28

Listening to the composer

AARON COPLAND

Aaron Copland has written a lot of music about America, much of it about the West. In some of this music, you will hear cowboy songs that Mr. Copland has borrowed to make the music sound more western. He has combined his own musical ideas with these cowboy songs in very exciting ways. *Billy the Kid* and *Rodeo* are two famous ballets with music by Aaron Copland. It is no wonder he has been called "the cowboy from Brooklyn!"

This is a scene from Rodeo. *You will hear a genuine fiddle tune in the section called "Hoedown."*

My Aunt Jane (The Wee Shop)

Words by Richard Hayward   Irish Folk Tune
Adapted by Richard Hayward

Aunt Jane has an answer to "trick or treat."

1. My   Aunt   Jane, ___   she   brought me   in,
2. My   Aunt   Jane   has   a   bell   at the   door,
3. My   Aunt   Jane, ___   she's   aw - ful   smart,

She   gave   me   tea   out   of   a   wee   tin,
A   white   step   stone   and   a   clean   swep'   floor,
She   bakes   a   ring   in   an   ap - ple   tart.

Refrain

Half   a   bap   and   a   wee   snow   top,
Can - dy   apples   and ___   hard   green   pears,
When   that   Hal - low - een   comes round,

Three   black   lumps   out   of   her   wee   shop.
And   con - ver - sa - tion ___   loz - eng - ers.
For - nenst   that   tart ___   I'm   al - ways   found.

The tonal center (F) is in the first space of the staff. On what step of the scale does the refrain begin?

Play the refrain on the tuned bells or on the piano.

30

Old Abram Brown

Benjamin Britten

Take turns playing the pattern below (starting on D) on the tuned bells or on the piano while the class sings the song. Notice that the octave pattern starts on a downbeat, although the song starts on an upbeat.

Old A - bram Brown is dead and gone,

We'll nev - er see him more.

He used to wear an old gray coat

All but - toned down be - fore.

Words from "Tom Tiddler's Ground" by Walter de la Mare. Copyright 1936, Boosey & Co., Ltd.

You can conduct as you sing. Pretend that a string is stretched in front of you from the desk top to the ceiling. To start the song, slip the fingers of one hand up the string, come down and touch the desk on the first strong beat. Let your hand bounce a little, but get back up the string for the second beat. The hand comes down again for the next strong beat.

31

HALLOWE'EN
INDIGNATION
MEETING

A sulky witch
    and a surly cat
And a scowly owl
    and a skeleton sat
With a grouchy ghost
    and a waspish bat,
And angrily snarled
    and chewed the fat.

It seems they were
    all upset and riled
That they couldn't frighten
    the Modern Child,
Who was much too knowing
    and much too wild
And considered Hallowe'en
    spooks too mild.

Said the witch, "They call this
    the *human* race.
Yet the kiddies inhabit
    Outer Space;
They bob for comets,
    and eat ice cream
From flying saucers,
    to get up steam!"

"I'm a shade of my former self,"
    said the skeleton.
"I shiver and shake
    like so much gelatine,
Indeed I'm a pitiful
    sight to see —
I'm scareder of *kids*
    than they are of *me!*"

MARGARET FISHBACK

The Little Barn Owl

English Words by Margaret Marks   Robert Schumann

This song is one of many that Robert Schumann, a famous German composer, wrote for children.

1. I'm just a lit-tle barn owl Who has no place to fly.
   like to try my wings out In for-ests green and bright,
   say I bring mis-for-tune, And chil-dren fear my cry.

So lone-ly and for-sak-en, All night I hoot and cry.
To hear the lark at morn-ing, The night-in-gale at night;
They drive me from the raft-ers, Al-though I don't know why.

I'm doomed to spend my drear-y _ life In this old_
To see the fields in sum-mer-time, To feel the_
I'm sor-ry if I fright-en _ them, But I must_

mus-ty barn, Poor lit-tle barn ____ owl! 2. I'd
win-ter sun, Poor lit-tle barn ____ owl! 3. They
hoot and howl! Poor lit-tle barn ____

owl!

33

A composer must build a composition with as much care as a stoneworker uses in building a sturdy wall.

The first "stone" in Franz Joseph Haydn's minuet is a rhythmic motive.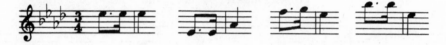

Haydn uses the motive many times in the minuet. How does he make the motive more interesting?

Sometimes Haydn separates the motives with rests.

Sometimes the motives fit closely together.

It is usually easy to hear when music reaches a "breathing place" and then moves on. A phrase is the music that you hear between these breathing places.

This diagram shows you how Haydn built his minuet of phrases and musical sentences:

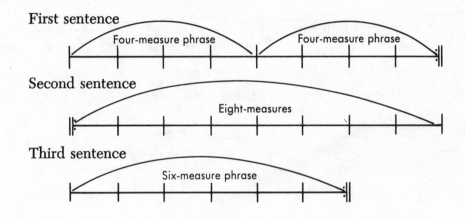

First sentence

Four-measure phrase   Four-measure phrase

Second sentence

Eight-measures

Third sentence

Six-measure phrase

MINUET NO. 1 (from SONATA IN A♭)

Franz Joseph Haydn

Away for Rio!

Sea Shantey

Long ago, people traveled over the ocean in sailing ships. To start the journey, the anchor was pulled up and the sails were hoisted.

Solo

1. Oh, the an - chor is weighed and the sails they are set,
2. We've a jol - ly good ship and a jol - ly good crew,
3. Oh, __ say, were you ev - er in Ri - o Grande?

Chorus

A - way _____ for Ri - o!

Solo

The gals that we're leav - ing we'll nev - er for - get,
A jol - ly good mate and a good skip - per too,
It's there that the riv - ers run down gold - en sand,

Chorus

For we're bound for Ri - o Grande! __

Refrain
Chorus

And a - way __ for Ri - o! Aye __ for Ri - o!

Solo

So fare ye well, __ my bon - ny young girl,

36

Chorus

We are bound for Ri - o Grande! _____

With your classmates, stand in a line ready to pull on a make-believe rope while a shanteyman sings the solo parts. On the chorus parts, everyone will sing and pull together. You will make two motions, one pulling and one releasing. The movement is pictured this way:

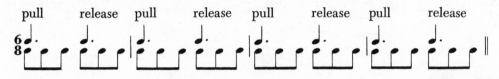

pull   release pull   release pull   release pull   release

The meter sign $\frac{6}{8}$ tells you that there can be six eighth notes in each measure. Find the measures in the song that are made up of six eighth notes.

The Sailor Fireman

Sea Shantey

1. I fired this trip, but I'll fire no more,
2. Miss *Nan - cy Bell*, oh, _____ fare you well, O - ho, O - ho, Oh!
3. Says I, "Old boat, let's _____ have no tricks,"

I'll take my mon - ey and I'll go on shore,
I'll take my mon - ey and I'll go on shore, Fire _____ down be - low!
Her boil - er burst _____ at _____ half past six.

From the book SHANTIES FROM THE SEVEN SEAS collected by Stan Hugill.
©1961, Stan Hugill. Reprinted by permission of E. P. Dutton & Co., Inc., and Routledge & Kegan Paul, Ltd.

Now Let Me Fly

Spiritual

Let your voice soar when you sing this song.

Refrain

Now let me fly, _____ Now let me fly, _____

Now let me fly _____ way up high, _____

Way in the mid - dle of the air.

Verse

Way down yon - der in the mid - dle of the field,

See me work - ing at the char - iot wheel.

Not so par - tic - 'lar 'bout work - ing at the wheel,

But I just want to see how the char - iot feels.

The refrain of this song is written for two groups to sing.
Study the notation. It will help you to sing either part.

Ezekiel Saw the Wheel

Spiritual

E - zek - iel saw the wheel,

'Way up in the mid- dle of the air.

E - zek - iel saw the wheel,

'Way in the mid - dle of the air.

39

La calle ancha

Folk Song from Puerto Rico

Girls and boys in Puerto Rico play instruments with their songs. When they play maracas, they make their hands dance.

Maracas

L   R   L   Shake

Play the maracas pattern throughout the song as an accompaniment. In the second measure of the pattern, shake both maracas, moving your arms up and down as you play.

Play as an introduction and continue throughout:

1. La ca - lle an - cha, cha, cha de San Ber - nar - do, do, do
2. Los cua - tro ca - ños, ños, ños dan a - gua her - mo - sa, sa, sa

Tie - ne u - na fuen - te, te, te con cua - tro ca - ños, ños, ños.
Pa - ra los ni - ños, ños, ños de Za - ra - go - za, za, za.

To conduct this song, you must show three beats in each measure. The first beat is shown by a downward movement. The second beat is shown by a movement to the outside — away from the body. For the third beat, the hand moves up in the air, ready to come down for the next strong beat.

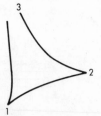

40

San Sereni

English Version by Delia Ríos   Latin-American Folk Song

This is a song about occupations.

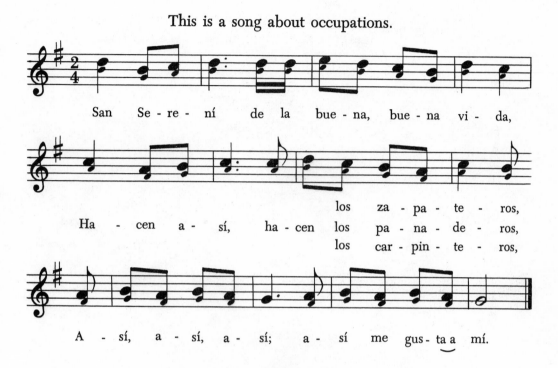

San Se - re - ní   de la bue - na, bue - na vi - da,

los za - pa - te - ros,

Ha - cen a - sí, ha - cen los pa - na - de - ros,
los car - pin - te - ros,

A - sí, a - sí, a - sí; a - sí me gus - ta a mí.

1. San Sereni, I'm a busy *zapatero*,
   Working like this to make some good *zapatos*,
   A-working just like this, a-working just like that.

2. ... *panadero*, ...
   ... bake ... *pancitos*, ...

3. ... *carpintero*, ...
   ... build ... *casitas*,

You can sing about other workers: *las lavanderas* — the washer-women; *las costureras* — the seamstresses.

When you know the song, take turns playing the second part on the tuned bells or on the recorder.

FRENCH

Isn't it strange
That in Paris
You are Vous
And Moi is Me,
And No and Yes
Are Non and Oui!

Isn't it odd
That in Bordeaux
Bread is Pain
And Water Eau,
And Good and Fair
Are Bon and Beau!

Isn't it queer
That in Calais
French *isn't* French,
And *is* Français!
What sort of French
Can that be, pray?

ELEANOR FARJEON

J'ai perdu le do (I Have Lost the *Do*)

French Folk Song

J'ai per - du le do de ma cla - ri - net - te,
I have lost the do on my clar - i - net, oh,

42

J'ai per - du le mi de ma cla - ri - net - te.
I have lost the mi on my clar - i - net, oh,

Sol sol la sol fa mi fa fa fa fa,

Fa fa sol fa mi re mi mi mi mi, Sol

mi mi mi mi sol mi mi mi mi sol la sol fa mi fa, Fa

re re re re fa re re re re fa sol fa mi re do.

Just as people in France have a language different from ours, so music has its own language for each step of the scale: do—re—mi—fa—sol—la—ti—do.

In the first phrase of this song, you sing the syllable "do." In the second phrase, you sing the syllable "mi."

How many phrases are there in this song?

The first phrase begins on "do." The second phrase, which begins on "mi," is like the first phrase in rhythm and melodic contour. Phrase two is a sequence of phrase one.

Can you hear other sequences in this song?

43

Un petit navire (A Little Ship)

English Version by Margaret Marks   French Folk Song

People take their songs with them wherever they go. This ballad of the sea is popular in France and well known in Canada.

Look at the French words. Find the ones with extra syllables.

1. Il é - tait un pe - tit na - vi - re,
1. A lit - tle ship once went a - sail - ing,

Il é - tait un pe - tit na - vi - re,
A lit - tle ship once went a - sail - ing,

Qui n'a - vait ja - ja - ja - mais na - vi - gué,
But on the o - o - o - cean lost its way,

Que n'a - vait ja - ja - ja - mais na - vi - gué, O - hé, o - hé!
But on the o - o - o - cean lost its way,

2. Au bout de cinq à six semaines *(2 times)*
   Les vivres vin-vin-vinrent à manquer. *(2 times)*
   Ohé, ohé!

   > 2. *And after weeks and weeks of sailing* (2 times)
   >   *There were no ra-ra-rations left one day.* (2 times)
   >   Ohé, ohé!

3. On tira à la courte paille
   Pour savoir qui, qui, qui serait mangé.

   > 3. *The crew drew lots to choose the sailor*
   >   *Whom they should ea-ea-eat for* déjeuner.

4. Le sort tomba sur le plus jeune:
   C'est donc lui qui, qui, qui fut désigné.

   > 4. *The choice fell on the youngest sailor,*
   >   *He was the one, one, one they would* sauté.

5. On cherche alors à quelle sauce
   Le pauvre enfant-fant-fant serait mangé.

   > 5. *And while they argued how to serve him,*
   >   *With lemon sau-sau-sauce or* Bordelaise,

6. Des p'tits poissons dans le navire
   Sautèrent par, par, par milliers.

   > 6. *A hundred thousand flying fishes*
   >   *Jumped on the de-de-deck and there they lay.*

7. On les prit, on les mit à frire
   Le jeune mou-mou-mousse fut sauvé.

   > 7. *And so the sailors ate the fishes.*
   >   *The boy was sa-sa-saved, oh happy day!*

8. Si cette histoire vous amuse
   Nous allons la-la-la recommencer.

   > 8. *If you've enjoyed this little ditty*
   >   *We'll sing it o-o-over right away.*

Notice how *"Ohé, ohé!"* is tacked on at the end of the four short phrases.

Can you hear the sequences?

LISTENING TO WOODWIND INSTRUMENTS

The flute, oboe, clarinet, and bassoon are members of the wood-wind family. All the instruments of this family were originally made of wood. Today the flute and sometimes the clarinet are made of metal or other material. The woodwind instruments are played by blowing across or into the tube of the instrument. The air column inside the tube is set in vibration, and tones are produced. As with the brass instruments, different pitches are created by changing the length of the column of air. This is done by covering holes (bored into the tube) with the fingers or padded keys.

The flute is the only woodwind that has no separate mouthpiece. The player blows across a hole near one end of the tube. The piccolo is a small-sized flute that sounds an octave above the flute.

The clarinet has a beaked mouthpiece with a single cane reed attached to it. The oboe and the bassoon are called double-reed instruments. The mouthpiece of each consists of two reeds tied together.

Look at the pictures of these five woodwinds. Which one produces the highest tones? Which one produces the lowest tones? How do you know?

As you listen to the following composition, try to match the sound of the woodwind instruments with their pictures.

Chasse à Valabre... Darius Milhaud

Chasse à Valabre, composed for a woodwind quintet, is a musical description of a hunting party. Listen for the hunting calls. In this composition, the bassoon (the lowest-sounding woodwind) plays sounds that are like the panting of a hunted animal.

In the following composition for three woodwinds, the bassoon plays a steady bass line (harmony part). This music does not tell a story. As you listen, try to follow the bassoon part.

Concerto in G Minor... Antonio Vivaldi

46

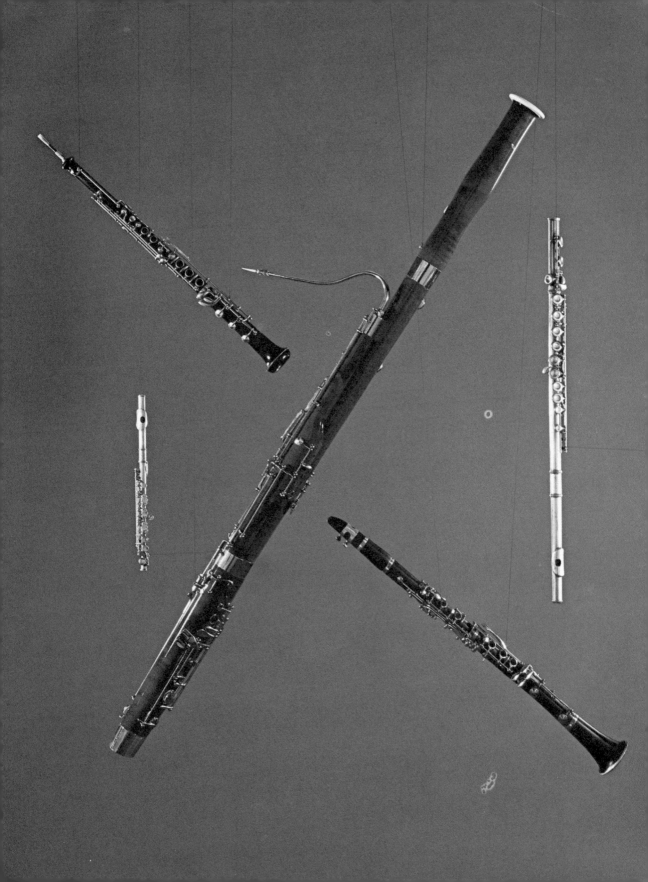

The Keeper

Old English Song

A man who takes care of a large estate may be called a "keeper."

1. The keep- er did a- shoot- ing go,
2. The first doe he shot at he missed;

And un- der his cloak he car- ried a bow,
The sec- ond doe he trimmed — he kissed; The

All for to shoot at a mer- ry lit- tle doe
third doe __ went where __ no- bod- y wist

A- mong the leaves so __ green, O.

Refrain

Jack- ie, boy! Sing ye well! Hey down,

Mas- ter! Ver- y well! Ho down,

From ONE HUNDRED ENGLISH FOLK SONGS edited by Cecil Sharp.
Copyright 1916, Oliver Ditson Company. Used by permission.

der - ry, der - ry down, A - mong the leaves so __ green, O. To my

A - mong the leaves so __ green, O.

hey, down, down, Hey, down,

To my ho, down, down, Ho, down,

der - ry, der - ry down, A - mong the leaves so __ green, O.

A - mong the leaves so __ green, O.

3. The fourth doe she did cross the plain,
   The keeper fetched her back again;
   Where she is now she may remain ...

4. The fifth doe she did cross the brook,
   The keeper fetched her back with his crook;
   Where she is now you must go and look ...

5. The sixth doe she ran over the plain,
   But he with his hounds did turn her again,
   And it's there he did hunt in a merry, merry vein ...

49

MAKING MUSIC YOUR OWN

RHYTHM

1. *Think* the tune of each of these songs: "America" and "The Star-Spangled Banner." Which one starts on a strong beat?

2. In what meter are both of these patriotic songs written?

3. Here is the melodic rhythm of two familiar songs. One is "For the Beauty of the Earth," and the other is "America." Name each song by looking at the notation of its melodic rhythm.

MELODY

1. Which one of the songs listed below begins on the tonal center? Which one begins on the fifth step above the tonal center? *Think* the tune of each song before answering the questions.

"Rarakatom!" "Come, Let's Dance"

2. How far can you go? Which songs listed below start on high 5, a fifth above the tonal center? Which songs start below the tonal center on low 5?

"Ezekiel Saw the Wheel" "San Sereni" "Hand Me Down"

3. Name the tunes.

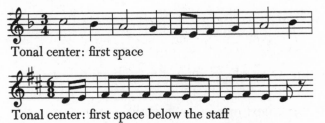

Tonal center: first space

Tonal center: first space below the staff

HARMONY

1. Can you hear the difference between the sound of the F chord and the sound of the C_7 chord? Sing as you listen to the chord pattern of "Skip to My Lou." The first chord you will hear is the F chord. Stand still when you hear the F chord. Move when you hear the C_7 chord. If you miss, you must sit down.

2. Play the game again with "Clementine." Sing as you listen to the chord pattern and respond to the chord changes as you did in "Skip to My Lou."

FORM

Can you match the two columns below? The names of three familiar songs are listed in one column. The names of three familiar forms are listed in the other.

1. "Come, Let's Dance"   1. AB
2. "Git Along, Little Dogies" 2. ABA
3. "Hand Me Down"   3. Round

To play three chords on the autoharp in the key of F, rest your index finger on the F button, your middle finger on the C₇ button, and your "ring" finger on the next button in that row, the B♭ button. Let your fingers seesaw between the F button and the B♭ button as you strum the strings. Listen to the sound of the B♭ chord.

Now strum the strings, once for each chord, as you press the buttons in this order: F, B♭, C₇, and F. Release one button as you press the next one. Practice until you can press the buttons without looking at your fingers.

Oh, Susanna

Stephen Foster

I came from Alabama With my banjo on my knee,
I'm going to Louisiana, My true love for to see;
It rained all night the day I left, The weather it was dry;
The sun so hot I froze to death; Susanna, don't you cry.

Refrain

Oh, Susanna, Oh, don't you cry for me,
I've come from Alabama With my banjo on my knee.

You need three chords to accompany "Oh, Susanna" on the autoharp. The B♭ chord is played in only one place — on the words "Oh, Susanna" in the refrain. When you know how the chord pattern fits the melody, sing the song and accompany yourself without looking at the notation or your fingers.

52

On Top of Old Smoky

On top of old Smoky,
All covered with snow,
I lost my true lover
A-courtin' too slow.

You can play an accompaniment for "On Top of Old Smoky", using three chords in the key of C — C, G₇, and F. Rest the tips of three fingers on the buttons for these chords and play them as you played the three chords in the key of F. Follow the notation and do not look at your fingers.

Red River Valley

From this valley they say you are going;
We will miss your bright eyes
    and sweet smile,
For they say you are taking the sunshine
That brightens our pathway awhile.

REFRAIN
Come and sit by my side if you love me,
Do not hasten to bid me adieu;
But remember the Red River Valley
And the girl that has loved you so true.

"Red River Valley" is in the key of G. The chords for its accompaniment are G, D₇, and C. The D₇ button is on the upper row, so your fingers will make a triangle when you play the three chords in the key of G.

Practice the chord pattern so that you can play without looking at the notation.

Who'll Buy My Fruit?

English Words by Margaret Marks   Czech Folk Song

Look at the notation to see where the chorus sings in two parts. The upper part starts on the fifth step of the scale. Where does the lower part start?

Who'll come this way and buy?

Who'll buy my fruit piled high?
         nuts

Peach - es, pears, and plums, and ap - ples,
Chest - nuts, wal - nuts, roast - ed al - monds,

Who'll come this way and buy?

If you try them, you will buy them.

Who'll come this way and buy?

In a market place in Europe, the vendor's cart is overflowing with fruits of the Fall harvest.

54

Chicago Street Cries

American Round

The vendors attract attention with their calls: "Potatoes, straw, morning papers, shine for your boots." Can you make your voices act out this scene as it would sound in a market place?

After you know the song, sing it as a round.

I
Po - ta - toes, ___ po - ta - toes, ___ Fif - teen cents a peck.

II
Straw, _____ straw, _____ Nice clean straw.

III
Here's your morn - ing pa - pers. Black your boots, Shine 'em up.

I've a Wagon

English Words by Margaret Marks   Dutch Folk Song

The wagon comes to market. Is this wagon loaded with vegetables?

This song has four phrases. What can you discover about them?

I've a wag - on full of 1. chick - ens / 2. duck - lings

Who are cack - ling and squawk - ing; / Who are flap - ping and quack - ing;

With my wag - on full of chick - ens / duck - lings

I would rath - er be walk - ing! / How my ear - drums are crack - ing!

It's cack - le, cack - le, cack - le, *squawk, squawk!* / It's pad - dle, pad - dle, pad - dle, *quack, quack!*

Melody reprinted from DUTCH FOLK SONGS by Coenraad V. Bos, copyright 1917, G. Schirmer, Inc.

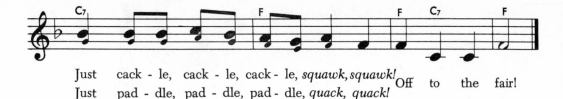

Just cack - le, cack - le, cack - le, *squawk, squawk!* Off to the fair!
Just pad - dle, pad - dle, pad - dle, *quack, quack!*

3. I've a wagon full of piglets
   Who are grunting and squealing;
   With my wagon full of piglets
   I've a terrible feeling!
   It's oinka, oinka, oinka, *snort, snort!*
   Just oinka, oinka, oinka, *snort, snort!*
   Off to the fair!

4. I've a wagon full of sweet hay
   Which is silent and golden;
   For my wagon full of sweet hay
   To the Lord I'm beholden!
   It's _____ *(silence)*
   Just _____
   Off to the fair!

For Health and Strength

Old English Round

Join hands with your neighbors when you sing this song of thanks.

For health and strength and dai - ly food We praise Thy name, O Lord.

SOMETHING TOLD THE WILD GEESE

Something told the wild geese
  It was time to go.
Though the fields lay golden
  Something whispered, — "Snow."
Leaves were green and stirring,
  Berries luster-glossed,
But beneath warm feathers
  Something cautioned, — "Frost."

All the sagging orchards
  Steamed with amber spice,
But each wild beast stiffened
  At remembered ice.
Something told the wild geese
  It was time to fly, —
Summer sun was on their wings,
  Winter in their cry.

RACHEL FIELD

We Gather Together

English Words by Theodore Baker   Traditional Dutch Tune

1. We gath - er to - geth - er to ask the Lord's bless - ing;
2. Be - side us to guide us, our God with us join - ing,

He chas - tens and has - tens His will to make known.
Or - dain - ing, main - tain - ing His king - dom di - vine.

The wick - ed op - press - ing, now cease __ from dis - tress - ing.
So from the be - gin - ning, the fight __ we were win - ning.

Sing prais - es to His name; He for - gets not His own.
Thou, Lord, wast at our side; ___ All glo - ry be thine.

3. We all do extol Thee, Thou leader triumphant,
And pray that Thou still our defender wilt be.
Let Thy congregation escape tribulation.
Thy name be ever praised!
O Lord, make us free!

America, the Beautiful

Katharine Lee Bates   Samuel A. Ward

1. O beau - ti - ful for spa - cious skies, For am - ber waves of grain,
2. O beau - ti - ful for Pil - grim feet, Whose stern im - pas-sioned stress
3. O beau - ti - ful for pa - triot dream That sees be - yond the years

For pur - ple moun - tain maj - es - ties A - bove the fruit - ed plain!
A thor-ough-fare for free - dom beat A - cross the wil - der - ness!
Thine al - a - bas - ter cit - ies gleam, Un - dimmed by hu - man tears!

A - mer - i - ca! A - mer - i - ca! God shed His grace on thee
A - mer - i - ca! A - mer - i - ca! God mend thine ev - 'ry flaw,
A - mer - i - ca! A - mer - i - ca! God shed His grace on thee

And crown thy good with broth - er - hood From sea to shin - ing sea!
Con - firm thy soul in self con - trol, Thy lib - er - ty in law!
And crown thy good with broth - er - hood From sea to shin - ing sea!

59

LISTENING TO STRINGED INSTRUMENTS

The violin, viola, cello, and string bass are members of the string family. Although their shapes are similar, their sizes vary from small to very large. Violinists and violists hold their instruments under the chin. Cellists hold their instrument between the knees. String bass players must sit on high stools or stand to play their instruments, which rest on the floor.

Look at the pictures and tell which instrument plays the highest tones. Which instrument plays the lowest tones?

All the stringed instruments have a body made of wood, a fingerboard on a long neck, and four strings stretched across a bridge. Each instrument has a special bow that the player uses to set the strings in vibration. The bow is made of wood, with hundreds of fine horsehairs stretched from one end to the other. A string player draws the bow across the strings to produce a sound. Sometimes he plucks the strings with his fingers to play certain sounds. Plucking the strings is called playing *pizzicato*.

String players produce different pitches on the strings by shortening the length of the vibrating strings. Using the fingers of the left hand, the player presses on the string. As he makes the vibrating part of the string shorter, the pitch goes higher.

When you hear the following composition for a quartet of stringed instruments, listen for the difference as the instruments are bowed and as they are played pizzicato.

Canzonetta..Felix Mendelssohn

A string quartet is made up of two violins, a viola, and a cello. The string bass is not a regular member of a string quartet. When you hear the "Canzonetta" again, listen for the violins playing a melody with the viola and cello. The high and low instruments are playing in octaves.

EARTH AND SKY

(They talk to each other on Christmas Eve.)

Earth. Oh Sky, you look so drear!
Sky. Oh Earth, you look so bare!
Earth. How chilly you appear!
Sky. How empty you lie there!

Sky. My winds blow icy cold.
Earth. My flowers have gone from me.
Sky. Yet I've one Star of gold.
Earth. And I have one green Tree.

Sky. I'll set my Star on high
Alone in its own light
For any Child to spy
Who wakes on Christmas Night.

Earth. I'll hang my Tree with toys,
Like fruit and flowers gay,
For little girls and boys
To pick on Christmas Day.

They say
together. Then let the soft snow fall,
And let the cold wind blow!
We have in spite of all
A pretty thing to show;

Yes, Christmas Eve and Morn
We'll show our pretty thing
To every baby born
Of Beggar-man or King.

Earth. Oh Sky, you look so clear!
Sky. Oh Earth, you look so fair!
Earth. How bright your Star shines here.
Sky. How green your Tree grows there.

ELEANOR FARJEON

63

In many parts of the world, Christmas is celebrated over a long period of time. Celebrations begin four Sundays before Christmas Day and last until January 6 — twelve days after Christmas Day.

In Sweden, one of the Christmas celebrations takes place on December 13 to honor St. Lucia. On that day, the oldest daughter in every family pretends to be Lucia. She gets up early in the morning to prepare a breakfast of coffee and special buns for her family. She dresses in a white robe with a crimson sash and places a wreath of candles on her head. Then she wakens the family with a song and serves the special breakfast.

St. Lucia's Day

English Words by Alice Firgau   Swedish Carol

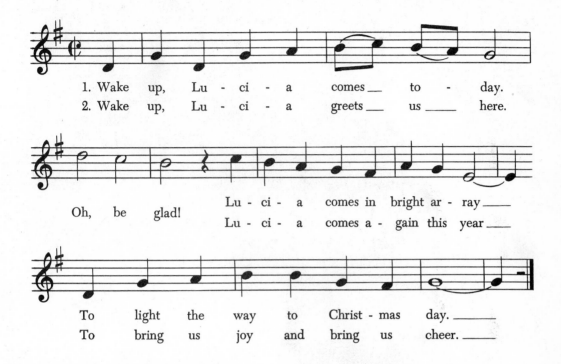

1. Wake up, Lu - ci - a comes___ to - day.
2. Wake up, Lu - ci - a greets___ us ___ here.

Oh, be glad!
Lu - ci - a comes in bright ar - ray___
Lu - ci - a comes a - gain this year___

To light the way to Christ - mas day. ___
To bring us joy and bring us cheer. ___

3. She enters with the morning light.
   Oh, be glad!
   Her happy face, 'neath candles bright,
   Dispels the darkness of the night.

4. This day our hearts are filled with love.
   Oh, be glad!
   Lucia tells of God's great love
   And of His Gift from heav'n above.

On December 13, Lucia and her family begin to get ready for the Christmas Eve celebration. They gather to make gifts for each other. Each gift must be beautifully wrapped, and a special verse must be written to go with each present. The verse will tell the person who receives it what he must do before he opens his gift.

As the days go by, the pile of presents to go under the Christmas tree grows bigger and bigger. The tree is behind closed doors.

65

On Christmas Eve the doors swing open, and there is the beautiful tree with its sparkling decorations! The gaily wrapped gifts are piled under its branches. Everyone joins hands, and as they sing they dance around the tree. They dance in and out of the rooms in the house, then back around the tree again.

Christmas Is Here Again

English Translation by Coleman and Jörgensen   Swedish Folk Song

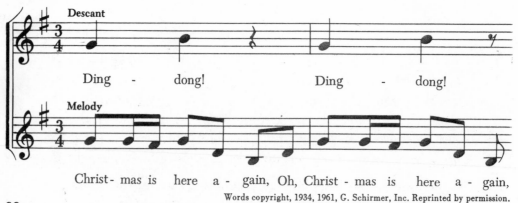

Ding - dong!   Ding - dong!

Christ-mas is here a-gain, Oh, Christ-mas is here a-gain,

Ding - dong, ding - dong!

Our hol - i - days will last till Eas - ter.

Ding - dong! Ding - dong!

Then it is Eas - ter - time, Oh, then it is Eas - ter - time,

Ding - dong! Ding - dong!

And Eas - ter joy will last till Christ - mas.

Hejom, Fejom

English Words by Ruth Tooze   Swedish Folk Song

After the dancing and singing, Father or one of the older children gives out the presents. As each person receives his gift, he reads the verse aloud and "pays the forfeit" before opening it.

1. Watch when you o - pen this gift so gay,
2. Shut your eyes tight when you o - pen this,

He - jom, fe - jom, fal - li - ral - li - ra.

For some - thing may jump out, then you can play,
To find a sur - prise that you must not miss,

He - jom, fe - jom, fal - li - ral - li - ra.

3. Hop on one foot and untie the string...
   Then you'll make us laugh as you dance and sing...

4. Mother, you must feed the birds today...
   Before you can open the wrappings gay...

Children in Sweden know the legend of Nissen, a little troll who lives in the barn most of the year. He likes to join the family on Christmas Day. Into the room he hops, bringing good wishes to everyone. Father thanks Nissen, then leads the family in a dance.

While everyone is dancing, Nissen disappears. But the children know that he will come back again on the next Christmas Day.

Then it is time to feed the birds so that they too may share the family's joy on Christmas Day.

Carol of the Birds

French Carol

1. Whence comes this rush of wings a - far,
2. Tell us, ye birds, why come ye here,
3. An - gels and shep - herds, birds of the sky,

Fol - low - ing straight the No - ël star?
In - to this sta - ble poor and drear?
Come where the Son of God doth lie;

Birds from the woods in won - drous flight
"Has - t'ning we seek the new - born King,
Christ on ____ earth with man doth dwell,

Beth - le - hem seek this ho - ly night.
And all our sweet - est mu - sic bring."
Join in the shout, "No - ël, No - ël!"

O Come, All Ye Faithful (Adeste, fideles)

Traditional

Throughout all of the festivities, beginning as early as St. Lucia's Day, Star Boys go caroling from house to house. Each one carries a pole that has a gold paper star fastened to the top.

1. O come, all ye faith-ful, Joy-ful and tri-um-phant,
1. A - des - te, fi - de - les, Lae - ti, tri - um - phan - tes,

O come ye, O come____ ye to Beth - le - hem;
Ve - ni - te, ve - ni - te in Beth - le - hem:

Come and be-hold Him, Born the King of An - gels.
Na - tum vi - de - te, Re - gem an - ge - lo - rum:

70

Refrain

O come, let us a - dore Him, O come, let us a - dore Him,
Ve - ni - te a - do - re - mus, Ve - ni - te a - do - re - mus,

O come, let us a - dore Him,___ Christ ___ the Lord.
Ve - ni - te a - do - re - mus ___ Do - mi - num.

2. Sing, choirs of angels,
   Sing in exultation,
   O sing, all ye citizens of heav'n above,
   Glory to God,
   All glory in the highest.

2. *Cantet nunc Io*
   Chorus angelorum;
   Cantet nunc aula caelestium,
   Gloria, gloria
   In excelsis Deo!

Christmas is a time for singing and feasting. There are treats for all the carolers.

We Wish You a Merry Christmas

1. We wish you a merry Christmas,
   We wish you a merry Christmas,
   We wish you a merry Christmas,
   And a happy New Year!

2. Now bring us some figgy pudding, *(3 times)*
   And bring it out here.

3. For we love our figgy pudding,   *(3 times)*
   So bring some out here.

4. We won't go until we get some,   *(3 times)*
   So bring some out here.

Carolers all over the world sing "Silent Night." You can play an autoharp accompaniment for it. Use this pattern:

$\frac{6}{8}$ ♩. ♩. *throughout*

C	C	C	C	G₇	G₇	C	C	
F	F	C	C	F	F	C	C	
G₇	G₇	C ___		C	G₇	C ___	‖

Silent Night
Joseph Mohr

Silent night, holy night,
All is calm, All is bright
Round yon Virgin Mother and Child.
Holy Infant so tender and mild,
Sleep in heavenly peace,
Sleep in heavenly peace.

Pat-a-pan

English Words by Janet E. Tobitt   Early Burgundian French Carol

Drum

Chant   pan pat - a - pan pat - a - pan pat - a - pan pat - a -

1. Wil - lie, take your lit - tle drum; Rob-in, bring your fife and come;

Play - ing   on   the   fife   and   drum,

Tu - re - lu - re - lu,   pat- a - pat- a - pan,

We'll make mu - sic loud and gay, For our Christ-mas hol - i - day.

2. Shepherds glad, in ancient days,
   Gave the King of Kings their praise;
   Playing on the fife and drum,
   Tu-re-lu-re-lu, pat-a-pat-a-pan,
   They made music loud and gay,
   On the Holy Child's birthday.

3. Christian men, rejoice as one,
   Leave your work and join our fun;
   Playing on the fife and drum,
   Tu-re-lu-re-lu, pat-a-pat-a-pan,
   We'll make music loud and gay,
   For our Christmas holiday.

Two Villancicos...Juan del Encina

73

The Coventry Carol

Robert Croo   Traditional English Carol
Descant by Mary Val Marsh

Lul - ly, lul - lay, Thou lit - tle ti - ny Child,

By, by, lul - ly, lul - lay.

O sis - ters, too, How may we do

For to pre - serve, this day,

This poor Young - ling for Whom we do sing,

"By, by, lul - ly, lul - lay"?

Can you tell why the first phrase of the finger cymbal pattern cannot be played throughout the song?

Finger Cymbals

74

Descant for recorder, bells, or voice

Sing "Ah" throughout.

Here We Come A-Wassailing

With the singing and playing of carols, the
long Christmas continues until Twelfth-night.

1. Here we come a-wassailing Among the leaves so green;
   Here we come a-wand'ring, So fair to be seen.

   Refrain
   Love and joy come to you, And to you glad Christmas too;
   And God bless you and send you a happy New Year,
   And God send you a happy New Year.

2. We are not daily beggars That beg from door to door;
   But we are neighbors' children, Whom you have seen before.

3. God bless the master of this house, Likewise the mistress, too,
   And all the little children That round the table go.

OTHER CHILDREN

Some children live in palaces
Behind an iron gate
And go to sleep in beds of gold
Whenever it gets late.

Some other children live in tents
With feathers all around
And take their naps in blankets
That are spread upon the ground.

And way up north the children live
In houses built of ice
And think that beds made out of fur
Are really very nice.

In countries where the nights are hot,
Without a single breeze,
The children sleep on bamboo beds
That fasten in the trees.

Some day I think I'll travel 'round
And visit every land
And learn to speak the language that
Each child can understand.

They'll teach me how to play their games
And, if they want me to,
I'll show them different kinds of tricks
That I know how to do.

They'll want to ask me questions then
And I will ask them others,
Until at last we understand
Like sisters and like brothers.

HELEN WING

From High Above

English Words by Alice Firgau   German Round

Look at the meter sign in this song. The sign C is another way of writing the meter sign $\frac{4}{4}$. Both signs mean the same thing — there are four beats in a measure and a quarter note is the symbol for one beat.

From high a - bove   The rain snow comes fall - ing, fall - ing down,

But soon a - gain the sun will shine And wear a — gold- en crown.

This song begins on the fourth beat of the measure — the upbeat. Look at the picture that shows the conducting motions for C, or $\frac{4}{4}$ meter. Notice that the song begins when the conductor's hand moves up in the air, ready to come down for the first strong beat.

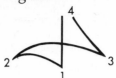

Conduct as you sing this song. When you know it, sing it as a round. Each part begins on the upbeat. The second part starts one measure later than the first part.

Peter, Go Ring the Bells

Spiritual

Refrain

Oh, Pe - ter, go ring the bells, Pe - ter, go ___ ring the bells,

Pe - ter, go ring the bells; I heard from heav - en to - day.

Verse

I won - der where my broth - er is gone,

I won - der where my ___ broth - er is gone,

I won - der where my broth - er is gone;

D. C. al Fine

I heard from heav - en to - day.

If you climb up a tree,
you must climb down
the same tree.

The horse that arrives
early gets good drinking
water.

By trying often, the monkey
learns to jump from
the tree.

Little by little
grow the
bananas.

From *African Proverbs* compiled by CHARLOTTE AND WOLF LESLAU

Onchimbo

English Words by Margaret Marks   African Folk Song from Kenya
As Sung by Ruth Nthreketha

Boys and girls who live in Africa learn the customs of their tribe
through singing and dancing. After supper, families gather outside their huts to act out the happenings of the day.

When you know this song, play a percussion part on the top of
your desk or on a drum. Scrape the guiro during the quarter
rest in the drum part.

81

Johnny Lazybones

English Words by Margaret Marks   African Work Song from Kenya
As Sung by Mary Okari

Work songs, sung in the fields, are brought back to the community
to be acted out.

You can do a dance to act out the work. The men stand in a line
behind a leader. They take one step forward, make the motion of
digging with a shovel, then make the motion of throwing the dirt
over the left shoulder. A drummer can play as the men repeat
the motions over and over again.

82

Rise and Stretch

English Words by Margaret Marks   African Work Chant

The workers stand in rows. They bend to clear brush and gather
sticks for fuel. When the water carrier appears, the workers who
see him first stand up and call to the workers in the next row. The
news is called from row to row.

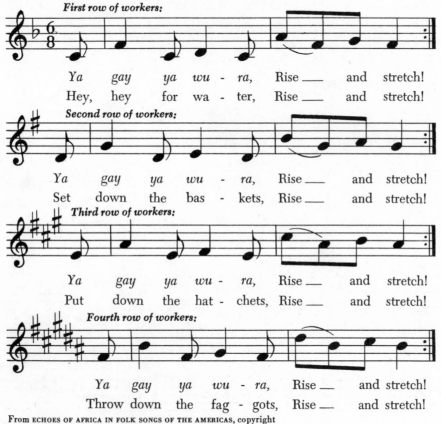

First row of workers:

Ya   gay   ya   wu - ra,   Rise ___   and   stretch!
Hey,   hey   for   wa - ter,   Rise ___   and   stretch!

Second row of workers:

Ya   gay   ya   wu - ra,   Rise ___   and   stretch!
Set   down   the   bas - kets,   Rise ___   and   stretch!

Third row of workers:

Ya   gay   ya   wu - ra,   Rise ___   and   stretch!
Put   down   the   hat - chets,   Rise ___   and   stretch!

Fourth row of workers:

Ya   gay   ya   wu - ra,   Rise ___   and   stretch!
Throw   down   the   fag - gots,   Rise ___   and   stretch!

Act out the part of the workers. Drum parts will help your dramatization. Choose one to play throughout the song.

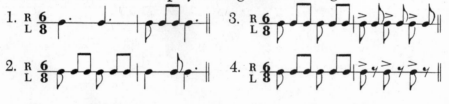

The Camel

English Words by Phyllis Resnick   Folk Song from the Middle East

Use a combination of these rhythm patterns to improvise an accompaniment. Play the accompaniment on finger cymbals or drums.

Get up, my cam - el, ____ for we must trav - el. ____

No more of rest and sleep, ___ now we must trav - el. ____

Make haste, make haste, my faith - ful cam - el, ____

For you and I have far to trav - el. ____

Make haste, make haste, my faith - ful cam - el, ____

For you and I have far to trav - el.

From Folkways Record #FC7226, Folkways Records & Service Corp.

Ala Delona

English Words by Alice Firgau   Arabic Folk Song

هذه احدى الاغاني العربيه الشعبيه
المشهوره في الشرق الادسط . مع أن الكلمات
تختلف من بلد الى بلد، النغم لا يتغير مطلقاً .
أديب مدانات

This is one of the famous Arabic folk songs in the Middle East. Although the words vary from one country to another, the melody is the same.

Adeeb Madanat

A - la De - lo - na, A - la De - lo - na,

Through the night the des - ert __ winds are sigh - ing.

Fine

Tell me where she's gone, My __ fair De - lo - na,
Dark and love - ly braids,

She is sweet and kind and __ brings such glad - ness.
Has she gone for - ev - er? __ Oh, what sad - ness.

D. C. al Fine

Melody by permission of Cooperative Recreation Service, Inc.

When you clap, cup your hands to make a hollow sound.

Clap

Tambourine

85

Raisins and Almonds

English Words by Sylvia and John Kolb

Jewish Folk Song
Descant by Mary Val Marsh

From A TREASURY OF FOLK SONGS ("Frankie and Johnny and Ninety Others").
Copyright 1948, Sylvia and John Kolb.

While moth - er her watch ____ will keep, ____

To bring you back rai - sins and al - monds. __

Sleep, my lit - tle one, sleep.

Lullabies are sung all over the world. Can you find the words that suggest in what part of the world this mother lives?

The melody of this song, as well as the descant, can be played on a recorder. The descant may also be sung as a second part.

To play an autoharp accompaniment in the key of D minor, place three fingers on the three buttons (d min., A₇, and g min.) ready to play as each is needed. Look at the notation, *not* at your fingers, as you strum.

Cretan Dance

English Words by Margaret Marks

Traditional Song from Greece
Collected by Adelina Ardittis

All the people who live around the eastern part of the Mediterranean perform their music in much the same way. Their instruments, their dances, and their style of singing are similar.

It's round a-bout and in and out Un - til the twi-light clos - es,

While breez - es from Mount I - da come To scent the air with ros - es.

1. There comes a day in ear - ly May Up - on the Isle of Crete, oh!
2. The girls of Crete are fair and fleet, The boys are strong and hand-some,

When danc - ing bands through-out the land Bring in the cher - ries sweet, oh!
As when of yore the Min - o- taur Would claim them for his ran - som.

3. Oh, long ago came Arab foe,
   Came Norman, Turk, Venetian,

   But hearts of Crete forever beat
   For freedom loving Grecian!

88

This song has two sections, A and B.

Play the finger cymbal pattern throughout section A. Clap hands on every beat throughout section B.

Finger Cymbals

In this composition, Jacques Ibert, a French composer, captures the mood of a Middle Eastern musician as he pipes a slow, sad melody:

Tunis-Nefta ....Jacques Ibert

Can you tell to which family the solo instrument belongs? Is it an oboe, cello, or bassoon?

When you listen to this composition again, follow the rhythmic accompaniment of the strings and timpani. The strings are played with the back of the bow. The wood striking the strings produces an unusual effect.

On another day, listen to the form of this piece. It is ABA. In section A, the solo instrument plays in its low register. Three repeated chords played by the strings introduce section B. In section B, the solo instrument plays in its high register. After a quick shaking back and forth on two notes and a slight pause, the melody returns to section A.

¡Qué bueno es saber tocar!

Spanish Folk Song   Collected and Adapted by B. L.

Each instrument has a solo part in this cumulative song. Take turns playing the solo parts when they occur in the song.

¡Qué bue - no es sa - ber to - car,

la tam - bo - ra!
la corna - mu - sa!
la gui - ta - rra!
el al - bo - gue!

Sa - ber to - car ___

(1.) Ram pla - ta - plám de la tam - bo - ra;
(2.) Cua - ra cua - cuá de la corna - mu - sa; (Repeat 1.)
(3.) Rau - - rau - rau de la gui - ta - rra; (Repeat 2 and 1.)
(4.) Tre - - re - ré ___ del al - bo - gue; (Repeat 3, 2, and 1.)

¡Sa - ber to - car, sa - ber to - car!

Look at the notation to see where the chorus sings in two parts. The tonal center is in the first space of the staff. The top part of the cumulative phrase starts on the fifth step of the scale. On what step of the scale does the lower part start? Both parts follow the same melodic contour, but a third apart.

90

SINGING IN THIRDS

Sing "San Serení," page 41. The song ends on the tonal center. Can you hear on which step of the scale the song starts?

Sing the song again, starting on the third step of the scale instead of the fifth step.

The notation for what you have just sung is the bell or recorder part written below the melody. The melody and the second part can be sung or played together in harmony.

When the class sings in harmony, it is especially important that each part begin on the correct pitch. Listening to the autoharp chords will help you to sing your part and will help you to sing it in tune.

Sing "La calle ancha," page 40. Notice that the song starts on the tonal center and moves to the fifth step of the scale on the first strong beat.

To sing a second part, start on the tonal center but move to the third step of the scale on the first strong beat.

Continue to sing the second part a third lower than the melody. The melody and the second part sung together will be in harmony.

Mañana

Spanish Folk Song

Collected and Adapted by B. L.

The tambourine score will help you to read the rhythm of this song because the tambourine plays on all the strong beats. Notice the places in the melody where a note on a strong beat is tied to the note that comes before.

When you know the song, learn the descant from the notation. Hearing the autoharp chords will help you. The tonal center is on the second line of the staff. On what step of the scale does the descant start?

La Tarara

English Version by Margaret Marks Spanish Folk Song
Collected and Adapted by B. L.

Flow-ers in a bas-ket on her head, Ta - ra - ra smiled and
Ap - ples

said, "Come buy some pret - ty red *flor' - ci - tas."*
man - za - nas."

Refrain

La Ta - ra - ra, yes, La Ta - ra - ra, no;

La Ta - ra - ra, yes, be - cause I love you so.

El payo (The Lazy Cowpoke)

English Version by Alice Firgau   Mexican Folk Song

The Spanish guitar is a popular instrument in Mexico. Use an autoharp to accompany this ballad. It will sound a little like a Spanish guitar.

1. Es - ta - ba un pa - yo   sen - ta - do ____
1. Oh, Nick, a sad, la - zy cow - poke, ____

En tran - cas de un ____ co - rral; _____
Would sit all day on a fence. _____

Y el ma - yor - do - mo le di - jo, ____
The fore - man saw him and told him, ____

"No es - tés tris - te, Ni - co - lás."_____
"Your sad - ness does - n't make sense."_____

"Si quie - res que no es - té tris - te_____
"Just give me all that I ask for_____

Lo que pi - da me has de dar."_____
And you'd cheer my low mor - ale."_____

Y el ma - yor - do - mo le di - jo,_____
The fore - man smiled then and told him,_____

"Ve pi - dien - do, Ni - co - lás."_____
"Well, start ask - ing, Nick, old pal."_____

2. "Necesito treinta pesos,
Una cuera y un gabán."
Y el mayordomo le dijo,
"No hay dinero, Nicolás."
"Necesito treinta pesos
Para poderme casar."
Y el mayordomo le dijo,
"Ni un real tengo, Nicolás."

2. "I need some thirty pesos,
A jacket, coat, and a hat."
The foreman smiled then and told him,
"No money have I for that."
"I need those thirty pesos
For to marry my sweet gal."
The foreman smiled then and told him,
"Do some work then, Nick, old pal."

How many phrases are there in this song? Which ones are alike?

Hello, Pretty Girls

English Words by Margaret Marks   Peruvian Folk Song

People from Spain were the first to voyage to South America.
On the west coast, high in the Andes mountains, they found an
Indian civilization known as the Inca Empire.

Clap this pattern throughout the song:

Boys 1. Hel - lo, pret - ty girls! With tight braid - ed pig - tails,
Girls 2. Go 'way, hor - rid boys! Your fin - gers are dirt - y,

Clean shin - ing fa - ces, Come out and play now!
Shirt - tails are flap - ping, Please go a - way now!

Don't sit in the court- yard Weav - ing your blank- ets.
Why should we be friend- ly When you're al - ways fight - ing,

It is gold - en sun - shine, Come out and play now!
Show - ing off and shout - ing? Please go a - way now!

Boys   3. Oh, please pretty girls,   We will stop our fighting,
              We'll clean up our fingers,   Showing off and shouting,
              Tuck in our shirttails,   We will treat you nicely,
              What do you say now?   What do you say now?

Girls   4. Oh, dear handsome boys,
              Did you say you'd treat us?
              Then we'll be friendly,
              We'll come and play now.
              We would like some corn cakes,
              We'd like some candy,

[*Girls* We will treat you nicely
[*Boys* They will treat us nicely

[*Girls* If you can pay now!
[*Boys* If we can pay now!

97

Sheep Are Grazing

English Words by Ruth Martin   Folk Song from Peru

In Peru the sheep graze on the steep slopes of the land.

Snow-white sheep are graz - ing   On the green hill yon- der.

Through the grass and clo - ver   Play - ful - ly   they wan- der.

Now the sun is set - ting,   Hear the shep - herd call- ing.

He   must lead them home-ward, Night will   soon be fall- ing.

After you know the song, follow the rise and fall of the notes on
the staff and play the tune on the black keys of the piano or on
the upper row of the tuned bells. Start on the first of a group
of three.

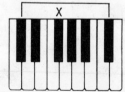

Notice that the notes of the tune stay within an octave.

98

IMPROVISING ON THE BLACK KEYS

Make up your own tune, using the black keys on the piano or the bars on the upper row of the tuned bells. Play your tune in one of the following rhythm patterns:

1. [rhythm notation]

2. [rhythm notation]

3. [rhythm notation]

Did you notice that your tune was complete and satisfying, no matter where it began or ended? There was no strong pull to a tonal center.

THE PENTATONIC SCALE

When you played your tune, you played groups of two and three black keys that make up the five tones of a pentatonic scale. Study the keyboard below to discover how a pentatonic scale is different from a major scale.

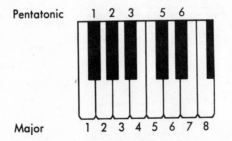

The tones that are missing in a pentatonic scale are *active* tones in a major scale. When any active tone is sounded in a melody, it seems to be pulled to a less active tone, as if drawn by a magnet. When active tones are missing, as in a pentatonic scale, the melody seems to "float." There is less pull toward a tonal center.

Dumplin's

Calypso Song from the West Indies
Collected by Massie Patterson

This is a conversation between Cookie and her friend.

You can use a drum part to accompany the second section.

The melody of this song uses the pentatonic scale. Play it "by ear" on the upper row of the tuned bells or on the black keys of the piano. The melody starts on the first of a group of two.

Find a partner to play one part of the conversation with you. In the first section, the first player (Cookie's friend) will use only the keys in a group of two. The second player (Cookie) will use only the keys in a group of three.

What happens in the second section?

Below is the notation for an American folk song you know. The tonal center, G, is on the second line of the staff. How does the song begin? Discover the tune by playing the first phrases on the tuned bells or on the piano. Play the rest of the song "by ear."

To make the tune sound like the one you know, you had to play F♯ (on the upper row) instead of F (on the lower row). What step of the G-major scale is F♯?

In a major scale, the seventh step is the closest one to the tonal center, 8 or 1. The tonal center acts as a magnet, drawing the *active* seventh tone toward it.

The fourth step of a major scale is an *active* tone, also. It is drawn to the third step of the scale. Look at the keyboard. Why is it unnecessary to change C, the fourth step of the G-major scale?

Play the tune above in the key of F. Look at the keyboard. Is the seventh step the closest one to the tonal center, F? Will the fourth step be played on the upper row or on the lower row to be close to the third step?

CHORD PROGRESSION

Take turns playing this chord pattern on the autoharp in the key of F. Listen to hear how each chord is related to the others. Your index finger will rest on I, your middle finger on V_7, and your ring finger on IV. Press and release the buttons as needed.

In the key of F, the F chord, or the I chord, is built on the first step of the scale.

On which step of the scale is the C_7, or V_7, chord built?

On which step of the scale is the B♭, or IV, chord built?

IMPROVISING WITH YOUR VOICE

As you listen to the chord pattern above played on the autoharp, improvise your own tune and sing it along with the autoharp accompaniment. Your tune will harmonize with other tunes that are sung at the same time.

On another day, improvise a tune using the chord pattern above. But this time, play the pattern in the key of C. Then improvise a tune using the pattern in the key of G.

This chant has a free rhythm that cannot be measured into regular groups of beats. Notice that it does not have regular bar lines or a meter signature.

Sán - - ctus, Sán - ctus, Sán - - - - - ctus.

Dó - mi - nus Dé - us Sá - ba - oth. Plé - ni — sunt coé - li et tér - ra

Your eyes and ears tell you that this music is measured into groups of two beats.

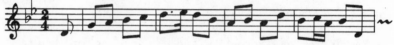

You have learned that the top number of the meter signature ¾ indicates that there are three beats in a measure. The bottom number indicates that a quarter note receives one beat.

The pattern that conductors usually use when they conduct music in ¾ meter looks like this:

Music in ⅜ meter that moves slowly is conducted with this pattern:

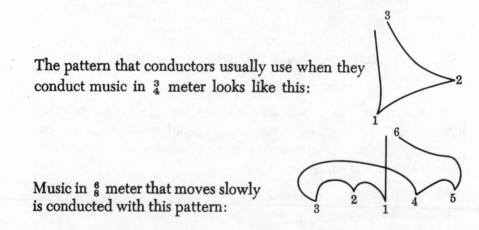

104

In some $\frac{7}{8}$ music, each measure is made up of a group of four beats followed by a group of three beats.

Here is a percussion composition you might play in your classroom:

This composition will sound different if you change the tempo. Try a slower tempo, then a faster one.

Experiment with dynamics. One player can play loudly while the others play quietly. All players can begin quietly and become gradually louder.

Choosing different combinations of instruments will also give the composition variety.

Charlie Is My Darling

Scottish Folk Song

Bonny Prince Charlie, an English prince, is a well-known hero in the British Isles. This song tells about his triumphal entry into the heart of Scotland.

Refrain

Oh, Char - lie is my dar - ling, my dar - ling, my dar - ling!

Char - lie is my dar - ling, the young chev - a - lier.

Verse

1. 'Twas on a Mon - day morn - ing,
2. As he came march - ing up the street
3. With High - land bon - nets on their heads

Right ear - ly in the year,
The pipes played loud and clear,
And clay - mores bright and clear,

When Char - lie came to our _____ town,
And all the folks came run - ning out,
They came to fight for Scot - land's right

The _____ young _____ chev - a - lier.
To _____ meet the chev - a - lier.
And the young _____ chev - a - lier.

Refrain

Oh, Char - lie is my dar - ling, my dar - ling, my dar - ling!

Char - lie is my dar - ling, the young chev - a - lier.

This song has two sections, A and B. What is the form?

Over the Sea to Skye

Robert Louis Stevenson   Annie MacLeod

Because of trouble on the mainland, Bonny Prince Charlie fled to the island of Skye.

Sing me a song of a lad that is gone,

Say, could that lad be I? _____

Mer - ry of soul he sailed on a day

O - ver the sea to Skye.

Verse

1. Give me a - gain all that was there,
2. Bil - low and breeze, is - lands and seas,

Give me the sun that shone! _____
Moun - tains of rain and sun, _____

Give me the eyes, give me the soul,
All that was good, all that was fair,

D. C. al Fine

Give me the lad that's gone! _____
All that was me is gone. _____

This song uses the pentatonic scale. After you know the song, follow the rise and fall of the notes on the staff and play it on the black keys of the piano or on the upper row of the tuned bells. Notice that the notes of the tune stay within an octave.

LISTENING TO THE ORCHESTRA

The string family is the backbone of the orchestra. The other instruments in the orchestra belong to the brass, woodwind, and percussion families. Among the percussion instruments are timpani, snare and bass drums, and other instruments that produce sounds when they are struck.

Listen for all the families of instruments as they play together in these two compositions:

Bourrée and Minuet.............................George Frederick Handel

The form of the "Bourrée" is ABAB. What family of instruments do you hear most in section A? What instrument announces the entrance of the full orchestra in section B? Notice that the tempo becomes slower at the end of the "Bourrée."

What is the form of the "Minuet"? Can you hear that trumpets play the melody in section A? What percussion instrument can you hear in section B? Listen for the musical conversation between the strings and the woodwinds in section B.

Handel composed this music for an outdoor spectacle, including fireworks and a hundred and one cannon salute. Although "Bourrée" and "Minuet" are pieces with dance titles, people listen to this music rather than dance to it.

Yankee Doodle

Dr. Richard Shuckburgh   Traditional

No one knows exactly where or when the tune of "Yankee Doodle" was first sung. We do know that many sets of verses have been written for the tune. Today the best known verse is:

Yankee Doodle came to town
Riding on a pony,
Stuck a feather in his cap
And called it macaroni.

1. ⅞ Fath'r and   I   went   down   to   camp,
2. And   there   we   saw   a   thou - sand   men
3. And   there   was   Cap - tain   Wash - ing - ton

A - long   with   Cap - tain   Good - in',
As   rich   as   Squire ___   Da - vid;
Up - on   a   slap - ping   stal - lion,

And   there   we   saw   the   men   and   boys
And   what   they   wast - ed   ev - 'ry   day,
A - giv - ing   or - ders   to   his   men;

As   thick   as   hast - y   pud - din'.
I   wish   it   could   be   sav - ed.
I   guess   there   was   a   mil - lion.

Refrain

Yan - kee Doo- dle, keep it up, Yan - kee Doo- dle dan - dy,

Mind the mu - sic and the step And with the girls be hand - y.

4. And then the feathers on his head,
   They looked so very fine, ah!
   I wanted peskily to get
   To give to my Jemima.

5. And there I saw a swamping gun,
   Large as a log of maple,
   Upon a mighty little cart;
   A load for father's cattle.

6. And every time they fired it off,
   It took a horn of powder;
   It made a noise like father's gun
   Only a nation louder.

7. And there I saw a little keg,
   Its head all made of leather,
   They knocked upon't with little sticks
   To call the folks together.

8. The troopers, too, would gallop up
   And fire right in our faces;
   It scared me almost half to death
   To see them run such races.

9. It scared me so I hooked it off,
   Nor stopped, as I remember,
   Nor turned about till I got home,
   Locked up in mother's chamber.

Take turns being a drum major to lead the parade. Here are two drum patterns to use with the song:

High drum

Low drum

Can you make up your own drum part? Can you show it in notation?

America

Samuel Francis Smith   Henry Carey

The words of "America" are set to a melody that has lived for many years. No one knows where the tune came from, but many people have used it — the Germans, the Swiss, the French. England's national anthem has the same melody.

1. My coun - try! 'tis of thee, Sweet land of
2. My na - tive coun - try, thee, Land of the
3. Let mu - sic swell the breeze, And ring from

lib - er - ty, Of thee I sing;
no - ble free, Thy name I love;
all the trees Sweet Free - dom's song;

Land where my fa - thers died, Land of the Pil - grims' pride,
I love thy rocks and rills, Thy woods and tem - pled hills;
Let mor - tal tongues a - wake, Let all that breathe par - take,

From ev - 'ry __ moun - tain - side Let __ free - dom ring!
My heart __ with __ rap - ture thrills Like __ that a - bove.
Let rocks __ their __ si - lence break, The __ sound pro - long.

4. Our fathers' God, to Thee, Author of liberty,
   To Thee we sing;
   Long may our land be bright With Freedom's holy light;
   Protect us by Thy might, Great God, our King!

114

God of Our Fathers

George W. Warren   D. C. Roberts

1. God of our fa - thers, whose al - might - y hand
2. Thy love di - vine hath led us in the past,
3. Re - fresh Thy peo - ple on their toil - some way,

Leads forth in beau - ty all the star - ry band
In this free land by Thee our lot is cast;
Lead us from night to nev - er - end - ing day;

Of shin - ing worlds in splen - dor through the skies,
Be Thou our Rul - er, Guard - ian, Guide, and Stay,
Fill all our lives with love and grace di - vine,

Our grate - ful songs be - fore Thy throne a - rise.
Thy word our law, Thy paths our cho - sen way.
And glo - ry, laud, and praise be ev - er Thine.

The Star-Spangled Banner

Francis Scott Key   John Stafford Smith

The tune of our national anthem was known in England long
before Francis Scott Key wrote his famous words.

Oh, — say! can you see, by the dawn's ear - ly light,

What so proud - ly we hailed at the twi - light's last gleam - ing,

Whose broad stripes and bright stars, through the per - il - ous fight,

O'er the ram - parts we watched were so gal - lant - ly stream - ing?

And the rock-ets' red glare, the bombs burst-ing in air,

Gave proof through the night that our flag was still there.

Oh, say, does that Star - Span - gled Ban - ner yet wave

O'er the land of the free and the home of the brave?

RHYTHM

1. *Think* the tune of each of these songs: "America" and "America, the Beautiful." Which one starts on an upbeat?

2. In what meter is it written?

3. Here is the melodic rhythm for the first phrase of two familiar songs. One is "Yankee Doodle" and the other is "¡Qué bueno es saber tocar!" Name each song by looking at the notation of its melodic rhythm.

MELODY

1. Sing the melody of "San Serení" to yourself. It has three phrases.

Which phrase starts on the fifth step of the scale?

Which phrase starts on the fourth step of the scale?

2. Which of these intervals is a fifth? a third? an octave?

3. You have played the following two songs on the tuned bells. Which one uses the pentatonic scale? How do you know?

"Down in the Valley"   "Over the Sea to Skye"

118

4. Name the tunes.

Tonal center: third line

Tonal center: first space

HARMONY

1. Can you hear how the sound of each of three chords (G, C, and D₇) is related to the others? Sing as you listen to the chord pattern of "Red River Valley." The first chord you will hear is the G chord. Stand still when you hear the G chord. Turn in place when you hear the C chord. Move forward when you hear the D₇ chord. If you miss, you must sit down.

2. Play the game again with "On Top of Old Smoky." Sing as you listen to the chord pattern and respond to the chord changes as you did in "Red River Valley."

INSTRUMENTAL MUSIC

Listen to two compositions based on the same idea—a hoedown. One composition is played by an orchestra. The other is played by instruments of one orchestral family. Which family is it?

Listen to two compositions for the orchestra. One features a solo instrument. The other features two orchestral families in dialogue. Which families are they? What is the solo instrument in the first composition?

THE PIPER

Piping down the valleys wild,
    Piping songs of pleasant glee,
On a cloud I saw a child,
    And he laughing said to me:

"Pipe a song about a lamb."
    So I piped with merry cheer.
"Piper, pipe that song again;"
    So I piped; he wept to hear.

"Drop thy pipe, thy happy pipe,
    Sing thy songs of happy cheer:"
So I sang the same again,
    While he wept with joy to hear.

"Piper, sit thee down and write
    In a book that all may read —"
So he vanished from my sight;
    And I plucked a hollow reed,

And I made a rural pen,
    And I stain'd the water clear,
And I wrote my happy songs,
    Every child may joy to hear.

WILLIAM BLAKE

121

NOAH AND THE ARK

The Lord told Noah to build an ark. So Noah and his sons built an ark and floated it on the waters. Then Noah took two of every kind of living creature — bird and butterfly, fish and snake, animals great and small — and led them into the ark.

Then the rains came. For forty days and forty nights it rained. It rained. It rained. The waters rose higher and higher and finally covered the earth.

Didn't It Rain!

American Folk Song
Collected and Adapted by B. L.

Did-n't it rain - a, rain - a, rain - a, rain - a, rain - a, rain - a, rain!

Did - n't it rain, chil - dren! My Lord, __ did- n't it rain! __

Oh, it rained for for - ty days and for - ty nights with - out stop-pin'.

Oh, it rained so hard that the wa - ter stopped a - drop - pin'.

Oh, did - n't it rain, chil - dren! My Lord, __ did- n't it rain! __

It was crowded in the ark. The animals kept Noah so busy that he often prayed:
"The days are long,
Lord.
Lead me until I reach the shore of Your covenant."

From "Noah's Prayer"

The animals prayed, too. The little foal prayed:
"Dear God,
when the strange night
prowls round the edge of day,
let Yourself be moved by my plaintive whinny;
set a star to watch over me
and hush my fear."

From "The Prayer of the Foal"

The little ducks prayed:
"Dear God,
give us a flood of water.
Let it rain tomorrow and always.
Give us plenty of little slugs to eat.
Protect all folk who quack
and everyone who knows how to swim."

"The Prayer of the Little Ducks"

The animals and every living creature became tired of the ark. They wanted to leave. But there was water everywhere. So Noah sent a dove to look for land.

The dove prayed:
"The Ark waits,
Lord,
the Ark waits on Your will,
and the sign of Your peace . . . .
The Ark waits,
Lord;
it has endured.
Let me carry it
a sprig of hope and joy . . ."

From "The Prayer of the Dove"

The clouds lifted. The sun shone. The dove returned bringing a small olive branch from land not far away. And once again, a man and his family and all the birds of the air and all the animals of the field and forest started life again on the good earth.

Quotations from PRAYERS FROM THE ARK by Carmen Bernos de Gasztold, translated by Rumer Godden. Copyright © 1962 by Rumer Godden. Reprinted by permission of The Viking Press, Inc., and Macmillan & Co., Ltd.

Open the Window, Noah

Spiritual

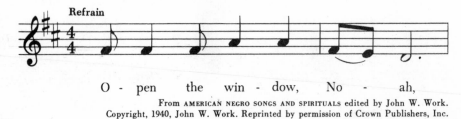

O - pen   the   win - dow,   No - ah,

From AMERICAN NEGRO SONGS AND SPIRITUALS edited by John W. Work. Copyright, 1940, John W. Work. Reprinted by permission of Crown Publishers, Inc.

O - pen the win - dow, No - ah,

O - pen the win - dow, No - ah,

1.,2.   Last time

O - pen the win - dow, Let the dove come in. dove come in.

Verse
Solo

1. The lit - tle dove flew in the win - dow and mourned,
2. The lit - tle dove brought back the ol - ive leaf,

Chorus

O - pen the win - dow, Let the dove come in.

Solo

The lit - tle dove flew in the win - dow and mourned,
The lit - tle dove brought back the ol - ive leaf,

Chorus   *D. C.*

O - pen the win - dow, Let the dove come in.

125

The Old Lord by the Northern Sea

Traditional Ballad

1. There lived an old lord by the north - ern sea,
2. One day they walked down by the wa - ter's brim,

Bow down, der - ry down dee,

There lived an old lord by the north - ern sea,
One day they walked down by the wa - ter's brim,

And down a der - ry down dee. _____

There lived an old lord by the north - ern sea,
One day they walked down by the wa - ter's brim

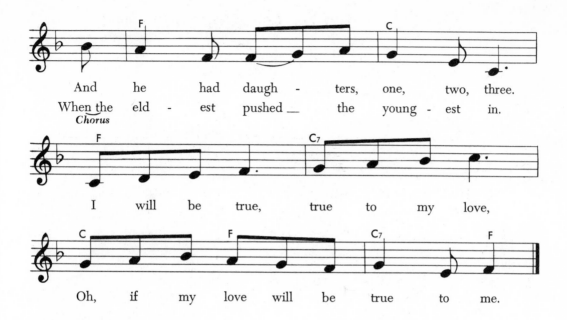

And he had daugh - ters, one, two, three.
When the eld - est pushed __ the young - est in.

Chorus

I will be true, true to my love,

Oh, if my love will be true to me.

3. "Oh sister, oh sister, pray lend me your hand,"
   Bow down, derry down dee,
   "Oh sister, oh sister, pray lend me your hand,"
   And down a derry down dee.
   "Oh sister, oh sister, pray lend me your hand,
   And I'll give you both house and land."
   I will be true, true to my love,
   Oh, if my love will be true to me.

4. "I'll neither lend you hand nor glove,"
    Bow down, derry down dee,
   "I'll neither lend you hand nor glove,"
   And down a derry down dee.
   "I'll neither lend you hand nor glove
   Unless you promise me your true love."
   I will be true, true to my love,
   Oh, if my love will be true to me.

5. So into the river the maiden swam,
   Bow down, derry down dee,
   So into the river the maiden swam,
   And down a derry down dee.
   So into the river the maiden swam
   Until she came to a miller's dam.
   I will be true, true to my love,
   Oh, if my love will be true to me.

6. The miller, he took out his rod and hook,
    Bow down, derry down dee,
   The miller, he took out his rod and hook,
   And down a derry down dee.
   The miller, he took out his rod and hook,
   And fished the maiden out of the brook.
   I will be true, true to my love,
   Oh, if my love will be true to me.

In "The Tides of Manaunaun," tone clusters are played with the left arm.

Listening to the composer

HENRY COWELL

Henry Cowell began writing music when he was very young. His first compositions were for the piano. They are not the kind of piano pieces we usually hear because Mr. Cowell was a composer who liked to experiment. He wanted to see just how many different sounds a musical instrument could make. He is shown here playing some of his piano compositions.

128

Mr. Cowell discovered a way to make the piano sound as gentle as an aeolian harp. His left hand silently presses the piano keys. Then he reaches inside the piano with his right hand and sweeps a finger across the strings.

Scary sounds come from the bass strings when Mr. Cowell sweeps his fingers over them.

129

IMPROVING ON THE BLACK KEYS

You can make up your own piano music for a play. Use the black keys and play clusters of tones with one hand as you play single tones with the other hand.

Make up your own story to tell through music or use one of the following ideas.

1. The North Sea on a stormy night
2. A peaceful farm by the North Sea
3. Animals going into the Ark
4. The dove finding land, then returning to the Ark with an olive branch

Think about your story as you play and try to find the tones that will tell it in the best way. The subject of your story will suggest the tempo (how fast or how slow) and the dynamics (how loud or how soft) that you will use in your music.

After you have spent some time experimenting at the piano, play your improvisation for the class.

There Was an Old Woman

Round

Sing this song as a round.

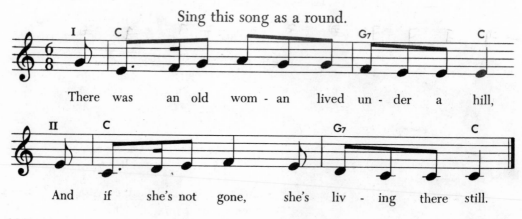

There was an old wom-an lived un-der a hill,

And if she's not gone, she's liv-ing there still.

130

The Wee Falorie Man

Irish Folk Song

People in the "north countree" will tell you that merry elves roam the land. They will tell you many tales about the elves' pranks and about their good deeds. The music shows you how this wee man's name is pronounced.

1. I am the wee Fa - lo - rie man,
2. I have a sis - ter, Mar - y Ann,

A rat - tlin', rov - in' I - rish - man.
She washes her face in a fry - in' pan.

I can do all that ev - er you can,
And out ___ she goes to look for a man,

For I am the wee Fa - lo - rie man.
Oh, I have a sis - ter, Mar - y Ann.

3. I am a good old workin' man,
   Each day I carry my wee tin can,
   A large penny bap and a clipe of ham,
   I am a good old workin' man.

4. I am the wee Falorie man,
   A rattlin', rovin' Irishman,
   I can do all that ever you can,
   For I am the wee Falorie man.

131

The Ninepenny Fidel

Joseph Campbell   Irish Folk Tune

My fa - ther and moth - er were I - rish,

And I am I - rish, too; _____

I bought a wee fi - del for nine ___ pence,

And it is I - rish, too. _____

I'm up in the morn - ing ear - ly

To meet the dawn of day, _____

And to the lint - white's pip - ing

The man - y's the tune I play. _____

For I'm up in the morn - ing ear - ly

To meet the dawn, the dawn of day,

And to the lint - white's pip - ing

The man - y's the tune I play. _____

In this song, notice the
patterns in ⁶₈ meter that
you know.

Find this new pattern:

Per Fiddler

English Words by Aura Kontra   Norwegian Folk Song

1. I know a young fel - low, Per Fid - dler's his name,
2. Per Fid - dler be - came the best fid - dler in town,
3. Per Fid - dler won't give up his fid - dle in trade,

I know a young fel - ow, Per Fid - dler's his name.
Per Fid - dler be - came the best fid - dler in town.
Per Fid - dler won't give up his fid - dle in trade.

He went in - to town with his cow for a trade
He played live - ly tunes so his friends could all dance,
And when he grows old, this is what I've been told,

And came back a - gain With a fid - dle well made.
He fid - dled the fid - dle when he had a chance.
He'll not swap his fid - dle for cow or for gold.

Refrain

Oh, fid - dler Fid - dler, play your fid - dle,

play your fid - dle, fid - dle - dee.

134

Paul and the Fox

English Words by Virginia Harrison   Norwegian Folk Song

There are eight phrases in this song. Which ones are alike?

1. Paul heard a noise, hur-ried out to the hen-house,
   Yelled at the fox, "Get a-way to the wild-wood,

   There saw a fox sit-ting down on his tail;
   Off to the woods, get you gone with-out fail!"

   "Squawk!" The hen to the chicks gave a warn-ing.
   "Squawk!" The hen sang her song in the morn-ing.

   Paul called his dog as he ran to the hen-house,

   Went for the fox as he sat on his tail.

2. Off ran the fox with the hen loudly crying,
   Straight to the woods where the foxes belong.
   Paul and his dog followed after a-flying,
   Caught Mister Reynard before very long.
   "Yap!" they met, and the fight soon was over.
   "Yap!" the fox was no match for old Rover.
   Off ran the fox, but the hen still a-crying,
   Back to her chicks went a-scurrying along.

PEER GYNT

Northern Europeans tell stories about elves, fairies, and trolls. According to old legends, these little creatures really exist. Henrik Ibsen, a famous Norwegian writer, wrote a play that includes an adventure with trolls. The hero of the play is Peer Gynt, a colorful character well known to Norwegian boys and girls. In one part of the play, Peer Gynt is surrounded by ugly trolls in their magical palace.

Edvard Grieg, a Norwegian composer, composed music for Ibsen's play. One of the pieces is called "In the Hall of the Mountain King." The music describes what happened in the palace of the king of the trolls. As the action becomes wilder, the music becomes more exciting.

The trolls are angry with Peer because he refuses to become like them and will not marry the Mountain King's daughter. From every nook and corner of the great hall, the trolls come to tease and bite Peer. They circle around him, growling and snarling. Peer tries to escape, but the trolls jump on him. Peer calls to his mother for help. Just then, the church bells ring in the valley and frighten the trolls away. The trolls shriek and shout as the hall falls to pieces and disappears.

In the Hall of the Mountain King......................Edvard Grieg

When you listen to "In the Hall of the Mountain King" again, notice that the same little tune is repeated over and over again to build up excitement. The music begins softly and mysteriously. The cellos and the string basses play the theme pizzicato. The bassoons play a staccato accompaniment. Can you hear the sequences in the music as the strings and oboe play the melody? Can you hear the cymbals crash? To what family of instruments do they belong?

The Judge's Ball

English Words by Margaret Marks   Swedish Folk Song

If you go to Sweden you may hear someone propose this toast:
"Your health, my health, a health to all the pretty girls." The
Swedish words for the toast are in the refrain of the song.

1. Now wear your fin - est gown And I'll drive you down to town
2. I'll hold your arm in mine As we're walk-ing in the line.

To a house on the old church square, oh.
Oh, the judge will ___ soon ap - pear, now!

We're go - ing to the hall For the judg - e's year - ly ball,
We'll walk ___ straight and tall With a smile for one and all.

All the pret - ty girls are there, oh!
Oh, the peo - ple all are here, now!

Refrain

Din skål, min skål! ___ Fill the bowl!

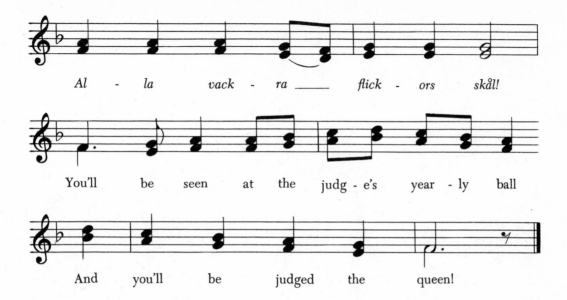

Al - la   vack - ra ____ flick - ors   skål!

You'll   be   seen   at   the   judg - e's   year - ly   ball

And   you'll   be   judged   the   queen!

This is a six-note tune that you can read from the notation to play on the tuned bells. The tonal center, F, is in the first space of the staff. It is the lowest note in the tune. What is the highest note? Find the frame these notes make on the keyboard.

Find F on the tuned bells. Play the first four steps of the scale in the key of F. Remember that the active fourth step is close to the third.

Now look at the key signature at the beginning of the staff. It tells you that the fourth step must be lowered to B♭ in the key of F.

The tune begins on the fifth step of the scale, C. Follow the rise and fall of the notes on the staff to see when they repeat, when they move up or down, and when they move by steps or skips.

When you can play "The Judge's Ball" in the key of F, play it "by ear" in the key of G. Will you use any bars on the upper row?

Play the same tune in the key of C. Will you use any bars on the upper row?

Play "Down in the Valley" in the key of F. It starts on the fifth step and moves up to the tonal center. From what you have played, can you tell what the key signature is for the key of F?

140

Petroushka

English Words by Margaret Marks   Russian Folk Song

Find the names of the Russian boys and girls in this song.

1. "Where _ is Pe - troush - ka, Pe - troush - ka?"
2. On ___ my ___ way I met Ko - lya

I _____ went ___ ask - ing near and ___ far.
With ___ his ___ bride - to - be, Ma - sha.

All up and down the town In the hope I'd track him down.
"Hey, Ma - sha! Hey, Ko - lya! Have you seen my Pe - troush - ka?

All up and down the town In the hope I'd track him down.
Hey, Ma - sha! Hey, Ko - lya! Have you seen my Pe - troush - ka?"

3. "We saw Petroushka, Petroushka
   In the park with Natacha.
   They're dancing hand in hand } (2 times)
   To the balalaika band!"

4. Who cares for Petroushka, Petroushka!
   I'll start dancing with Sacha,
   Vadim or Volodya, } (2 times)
   Toss my head at Petroushka!

Adieu to My Comrades (Fareweel to Tarwathie)

Scottish Folk Song

1. A - dieu to my com - rades, for a - while we must part,
2. Our ship is well rigged and she's read - y to sail,
3. The cold coast of Green- land is bar - ren and bare,

And like - wise the las - sie who's sto - len my heart.
Our crew, they are anx - ious to fol - low the whale;
No seed - time nor har - vest is ev - er known there;

I'm bound out for Green - land and read - y to sail,
Where the ice - bergs do float and the storm - y winds blow,
And the birds here sing sweet - ly on moun - tain and dale,

In hopes to find rich - es in hunt - ing the whale.
Where the land and the o - cean is cov - ered with snow.
But there is - n't a bird - ie to sing to the whale.

This song uses the five tones of the pentatonic scale. Play it "by ear" on the black keys of the piano.

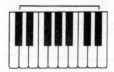

The song starts on the first of a group of three. The highest and lowest tones in the melody are within the frame shown above.

The fishermen say, when your catch is done
And you're sculling in with the tide,
You must take great care that the Sea Wolf's share
Is tossed to him overside.

From The Sea Wolf BY VIOLET MC DOUGAL

When the Boats Come In

Scottish Folk Song

1. We'll __ all be blythe and mer - ry when the boats come in,
2. There'll be lads and las - ses wait - ing till the boats come in,
3. Then __ Mag - gie, don your rib - bons when the boats come in,

We'll __ all be blythe and mer - ry when the boats come in,
There'll be lads and las - ses wait - ing till the boats come in,
Then __ Mag - gie don your rib - bons when the boats come in,

There'll be Dad - dy and our Jack, They'll __ both be com - ing back,
We'll __ go down to the quay, Your __ Dad - dy for to see,
Wash your face and braid your hair, For __ Dad - dy he'll be there,

With a catch o' bon - nie fish - es when the boats come in.
And __ glad he'll be to see us when the boats come in.
And __ blythe to see his lass - ie when the boats come in.

143

I'se the B'y

Newfoundland Folk Song

Not long after America was discovered, British fishing villages appeared along the rugged coast of Newfoundland. The people in these villages play this native Newfoundland dance at their community parties.

1. I'se the b'y that builds the boat, I'se the b'y that sails her.
2. I took Li - za to the dance; Faith, but she could trav - el.
3. Su - san White is out of sight, Hid - ing like Jack Hor - ner.

I'se the b'y that catch - es the fish And brings them home to Li - za.
Ev - 'ry step that Li - za took __ Covered an acre of grav - el.
Choose a lad and take __ him back, __ Kiss him in the cor - ner.

Refrain

Swing your part - ner, Sal - ly Tib - ble, Swing your part - ner, Sal - ly Brown.

Swing your part - ner, ev - 'ry - one, All a - round __ the cir - cle.

From SINGING HOLIDAYS by Oscar Brand. Copyright 1957, Oscar Brand. Reprinted by permission of Alfred A. Knopf, Inc.

People who live on the east coast of Canada often add a rhythm accompaniment to a song by tapping their heels on the floor. Can you tap your heels in the rhythm of this pattern as you sing the song?

PLAYING THE FIDDLE

Here is an arrangement of "I'se the B'y"
to be played on a violin:

The violin is tuned in fifths, starting with low G.

G D A E

Pick up the violin with your left hand and hold the wide part
under your chin. Pick up the bow with your right hand and
draw the bow across the two lowest strings, G and D. You will
be playing a fifth. Now draw the bow across the D and A strings.
You will be playing another fifth.

Play the pattern below as an accompaniment for "I'se the B'y."
Play the first line of the pattern as an introduction.

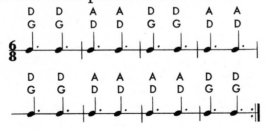

Listen to this composition for string orchestra:

Waltz ....Peter Ilyich Tchaikovsky

145

Mark you there yonder? With us once more. And lumps of blubber
There come the men Days of feasting Slapped down by the side bench?
Dragging beautiful seals To hold us together. Joyfully
To our homes. Know you the smell Greet we those
Now is abundance Of pots on the boil? Who brought us plenty!

From an Eskimo poem

Alaska, our forty-ninth state, is located in the northwestern corner of North America. It extends far out in the Pacific Ocean.

Northern Alaska has long been the home of the Eskimos. They live mainly by fishing and hunting or herding reindeer. As hunters, the Eskimos wander from one hunting ground to another in search of seals and other animals. They live and work together in small family communities and provide their own entertainment by making up poetry and songs.

The Returning Hunter

English Words by Elizabeth Whaley   Eskimo Song

When hunters return from a successful trip, they celebrate with their families. They accompany their songs by clapping hands, beating a drum or the cover of a large pan.

Boys
1. Sing the song of A - jung, Brave hunt - er A - jung,
2. Sing the song of Ka - lish, Keen fish - er Ka - lish,

Girls
3. Sing the song of Tee - ka, Bead - stitch - ing Tee - ka,

Brave hunt - er, bold and strong. Hunts for po - lar bear at night,
Keen fish - er, quick and true. In his kay - ak small and frail,
Bead - stitch - ing red on white, Sews a par - ka gay and bright,

Sends his spear in speed - y flight,
Braves the sea and wind and hail,
Mak - ing par - ka warm and light.

Hunt - ing car - i - bou, he shows no fright,
Spear - ing fish and ev - en gi - ant whale,
Sew - ing beads of red on hide of white,

O   A - jung,   Yai!
O   Ka - lish,   Yai!
O   Tee - ka,   Yai!

Click Go the Shears

Australian Folk Song
Adapted by Merrill Staton

Australia, the smallest continent, lies below the equator in the South Pacific. It is a land plentiful in wool and wheat.

1. Down by the pen, the __ old shear - er stands, _____
2. There sits the boss in his cane - bot - tomed chair in the
3. Shearing now is over and we've all got our checks,__ So

Grasp - ing the shears in his thin bon - y hands. __
middle of the floor with his eyes ev - 'ry - where, __
roll up the swag, boys, we're off to the next. The

Stead - y is his gaze on the sheep he's gon - na shear. __
Watch - ing ev - 'ry fleece as it comes _ to the screen, __
first __ chance we get we will all __ have a spree, So

He is al - ways hap - py when it's this time of year.
Pay - ing strict at - ten - tion that it's taken off ___ clean.
gath - er round to - geth - er now and join in with me.

Refrain

"Click" go the shears, boys, "click, click, click."

148

Wide is the blow and his hands are might-y quick.

Help hold the sheep now, — Don't let him kick. And

all the time the shears are go-ing "Click, click, click."

To make the clicking sound, play the rhythm of the melody on sticks. Notice when you play this pattern: ♩ ♫ Notice when you play this pattern, which gives a "jumpy" effect: ♩ ♩. ♪

149

I've Just Come from Sydney

Folk Song from Australia

1. I've just come from Syd - ney a - cross the range of moun - tains
2. Oh, how shall I find her? To you ___ I'll de - scribe her:
3. Oh, when shall I find her? She ran a - way with a stran - ger!

Where the nan - ny goats and the bil - ly goats and the moo - cows do dwell.
She ___ wears a flan - nel ___ pet - ti - coat and a hat up - on her head.
Fare - well ___ to the ___ nan - ny goats and the billy goats so high.

Oh, I've just come in search of a pret - ty lit - tle maid - en,
She ___ sleeps when she's walk - ing and snores ___ when she's talk - ing,
Fare - well to the moo - cows! By the sea - side I wan - der,

Though where she is now I can - not tell.
And her clothes are all marked with a "W, X, Y, Z."
And in its cold waters I'll lay me down and . . .

(**spoken**) *get up again!*

Collected by Hilda Lane, from POCKET SONGBOOK published by Edwards & Shaw, Sydney, Australia.

What is the meter of the autoharp accompaniment? On what beat does it start? Remember that a bar line is always placed before the first beat of a measure.

Can you discover why the last measure has only two beats?

Kookaburra

M. Sinclair   Round from Australia

Kook - a - bur - ra   sits   on   an   old   gum   tree, ___

Mer - ry,   mer - ry   king   of   the   bush   is   he. ___

Laugh, kook-a-bur-ra, laugh, kook-a-bur-ra, Gay your life must be.

From THE DITTY BAG, ©1946, Janet E. Tobitt.

Practice playing this melody on the tuned bells. Which phrase
is a sequence? What is the interval between the first note of
the first phrase and the first note of the second phrase?

Beautiful Hawaii

English Words by Aura Kontra   H. M. King Kalakaua

With the greeting *Aloha,* Hawaiians have welcomed newcomers to their islands from the East and the West. In Hawaii, people of different races and creeds live together peacefully.

Hawaiian music shows the influence of different cultures. Some songs are harmonized in Western style; other songs are like the chants of the Eastern countries.

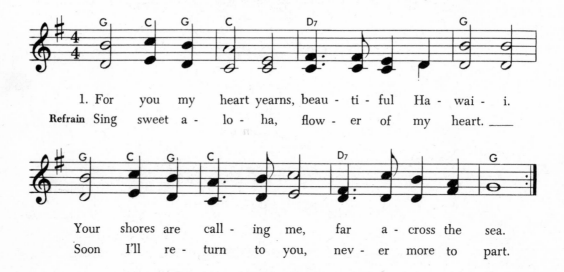

1. For you my heart yearns, beau - ti - ful Ha - wai - i.
Refrain Sing sweet a - lo - ha, flow - er of my heart. ____

Your shores are call - ing me, far a - cross the sea.
Soon I'll re - turn to you, nev - er more to part.

2. Climbing your mountains, sailing in the bay,
   I'll tell you of my love, dreaming cares away.

Accompany this song on a ukelele or strum on the right side of the autoharp to get the "ukelele" sound.

In this song, a phrase is four measures long. Study the chord pattern (shown by the autoharp symbols) of the first phrase. You will play the same pattern for phrase two.

Alekoki

English Version by Aura Kontra   Hawaiian Chant

A - o - le i pi - li - wi i - a,
Ho - o - ko - hu ka 'u - a i u - ka,

Ka - hi wa - i a - o A - le - ko - ki,
No - ho ma - i la i Nu - u - a - nu.

Oh, is there such a place of beauty
As the crystal pools of Alekoki,
Where forest shadows fall so gently
In the silence of the hidden valley?

"Alekoki" is one of many Hawaiian chants that is sung as people dance. The dancers hold a puili — a piece of bamboo that is fringed on one end to make the stick flexible.

Practice using a puili. Sit low on your heels and hold the solid end of the stick in your right hand. Strike the stick on the palm of your left hand, on the floor, on the back of your left hand, and on your right shoulder.

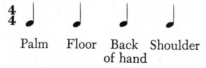

Palm   Floor   Back   Shoulder
             of hand

After you know the chant and the basic pattern of the stick, use it in a dance. Sit low on your heels, facing a partner, and let your body follow the movement of the stick.

Bento-Uri (The Lunch Vendor)

Japanese Vendor's Calls

As the train pulls into the Tokyo station, the vendors are wait-ing to sell the passengers a quick lunch. When you know the calls, sing them as a round.

O - ya - ko dom - bu - ri!   O - su-shi ben-to, san- do-wit - chee!

(Chicken and egg casserole)   *(Rice and fish sandwich)*   *(Sandwiches)*

La - mu - ne - ni, sa - i - da!   Gyu - nyu!

(Lemonade and cider)   *(Milk)*

Boys and girls in Japan play baseball, tag, hide-and-seek, and a game like badminton that they call *Hane-tsuki*. Before starting most of these games, children play a hand game — Jan-Ken-Pon — to decide on a leader or to choose sides. Two children face each other. Each one holds out a fist and shakes it in time to the chant. At the end of the chant, each makes one of these shapes with his hand:

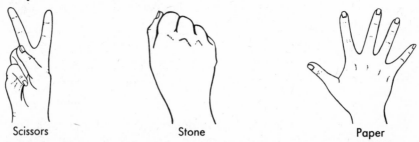

Scissors   Stone   Paper

Each hand movement can win or lose. Scissors can cut paper, so "scissors" will beat "paper." But paper can be wrapped around a stone, so "paper" will beat "stone." A stone can break scissors, so "stone" will beat "scissors."

Jan-Ken-Pon

Japanese Game Song

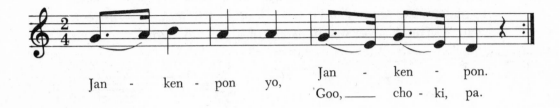

Jan - ken - pon yo,   Jan - ken - pon.
                        Goo,____ cho - ki, pa.

Rope-Skipping Chant

English Words by B. L. and E. C.   Game Song from Japan

Girls often play *Jan-Ken-Pon* while they are jumping rope and singing this song. Find the *Jan-Ken-Pon* melody in the song.

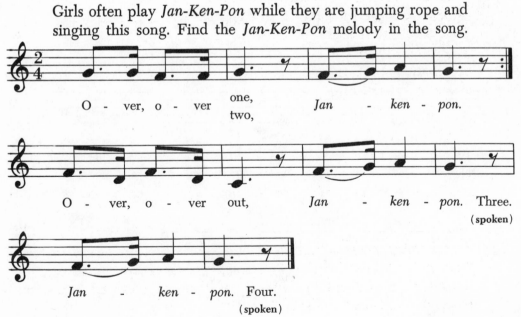

O - ver, o - ver one,   Jan - ken - pon.
                   two,

O - ver, o - ver out,   Jan - ken - pon. Three.
                                          (spoken)

Jan - ken - pon. Four.
              (spoken)

Sakura

English Version by Lorene Hoyt   Japanese Folk Song

"Sakura" is one of the first songs that children in Japan learn to play on the koto. The koto is a long instrument with thirteen strings. The player sits in front of the koto, which rests on the floor, and plucks the strings.

Play as an introduction and continue throughout:

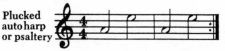

1. Sa - ku - ra, Sa - ku - ra, Cher - ry blos - soms ev - 'ry - where.
2. Sa - ku - ra, Sa - ku - ra, Blos - soms wav - ing in the_ breeze.
Sa - ku - ra, Sa - ku - ra, Ya - yo - i no so - ra_ wa,

Clouds of glo - ry fill the_ sky, Mist of beau - ty in the_ air,
Yo - shi - no, the cher - ry - land, Tat - su - ta, the ma - ple_ trees,
Mi - wa - ta - su ka - gi - ri, Ka - su - mi ka ku - mo - ka,

Love - ly col - ors float - ing_ by, Sa - ku - ra, Sa - ku - ra,
Ka - ra - sa - ki, pine tree_ grand, Sa - ku - ra, Sa - ku - ra,
Ni - o - i zo i - zu - ru; I - za - ya, i - za - ya

Let all come _ sing - ing.
Let all come _ sing - ing.
Mi ni yu - ka - n.

156

アメリカの少年少女の皆様へ

日本の古い童謡の一つで多くの人々に
親しまれている。この歌を皆様が唱えてくだ
さることをうれしく思います。いつかこの
桜の美しい頃、日本をおとずれて下さい。

東京都目黒区鷹番町四。

金井紘子
一九六四年度
I.C.Y.E 留学生

157

NAME THIS TUNE

Study the violin part in this instrumental arrangement. Can you discover what tune it is? It starts on the tonal center.

If you can play the violin or the piano, practice playing the melody or the accompaniment part at home so that you can play for the class. Find a partner to play with you.

LISTENING TO THEME AND VARIATIONS

Allegretto .... Gioacchino Rossini

You have heard how brass, woodwind, and stringed instruments are used in the orchestra or in small ensembles, or groups. An ensemble may consist of instruments of the same family, or it may combine an instrument of another family with the basic group. The "Allegretto" by Rossini combines the French horn with the flute, clarinet, and bassoon. Listen to the timbre of each instrument. Listen to the timbre of the four instruments as they blend together.

The form of the "Allegretto" is theme and variations. A simple theme is played first. Each time it is repeated, it is varied or changed. The theme may be varied by decorating the melody, changing its key, rhythm, mood, or tempo.

As you listen to the quartet again, follow the form of the piece. The flute and clarinet play the theme. The four variations that follow feature the other instruments. Can you tell which instruments play the four variations? After the fourth variation there is a finale, a concluding section that grows out of the last variation without interruption.

Theme

159

Spinning Song

English Words by Margaret Marks   W. A. Mozart

1. "Why must you spin so cease - less - ly?"
2. "Why must you spin so cease - less - ly?
3. "Why must you spin so cease - less - ly?"

Said hand - some Fritz, my neigh - bor.
Time, like your wheel, is fly - ing!
Said Fritz, with great de - vo - tion.

"Why don't you rest your eyes on me
If you would spend that time with me,"
"I'm ask - ing you to mar - ry me,

In - stead of on your la - bor?"
Said Fritz, "I'd stop my sigh - ing!"
So stop that cease - less mo - tion."

"Ah hand - some _ Fritz, I'll keep my _ wits,
"Oh, Fritz!" said _ I, "You sigh and _ sigh
And I con - fess that I said, _ "Yes,

Al - though your smile is win - ning.
Each new ro - mance be - gin - ning!
In that case I'll give in, sir!"

I know just _ what _ a _ flirt you are,"
But I'm not _ like _ those _ oth - er girls,"
And so, by _ spin - ning _ cease - less - ly

I said and kept on spin - ning,
I said and kept on spin - ning,
I ceased to be a spin - ster,

I said and kept on spin - ning.
I said and kept on spin - ning.
I ceased to be a spin - ster.

(Piano)

Ah, No, My Dear Mama

English Words by Nancy Rushmore   German Folk Song

Mother

1. "Come, An - na, Su - san - na, the fire you must set."
2. "Come, An - na, Su - san - na, and sweep up the floor."

Girls

"Ah, no, my dear Ma - ma, the wood is too wet."
boys knock at the door."

Refrain
All

Ru - di - ral - la - la la, ru - di - ral - la la la.

Ru - di - ru - di - ral - la la, ru - di - ru - di - la.

"Ah, no, my dear Ma - ma, the wood is too wet."
boys knock at the door."

Ru - di - ru - di - ral - la la, ru - di - ru - di - la!

3. *Mother:* "First polish the kettle and then you can prance."
   Girls: "Ah, yes, my dear Mama, we'll work then we'll dance!"
   All: **Refrain**
   "Ah, yes, my dear Mama, we'll work then we'll dance!"

4. *Mother:* "And if they can't dance, then I'll teach them to hop!"
   Girls: "She'll turn them about with a poke of the mop!"
   All: **Refrain**
   "She'll turn them about with a poke of the mop!"

When you know this song, take turns singing the mother and daughter parts. The class will sing the refrain.

Sing the melody of the verse by following the notation.

1. What does the meter sign tell you?

2. On what beat does the melody start?

3. The tonal center is on the second line of the staff. What is the interval between the first two notes?

4. Tap out the rhythm of the melody before you sing.

On another day, make the conducting movements for $\frac{3}{4}$ meter as you sing the song. Then walk in the rhythm of the meter. Step on every beat, accenting each strong beat by bending the knee. When you do this smoothly, you are doing a waltz-walk.

When you know the melody, study the notation to see where the chorus sings in two parts. Notice that in the refrain, the upper part starts on the third beat of the measure and the lower part starts on the second beat of the next measure. Each part begins on the same notes and with the same syllables.

163

May Day Carol

English Folk Song

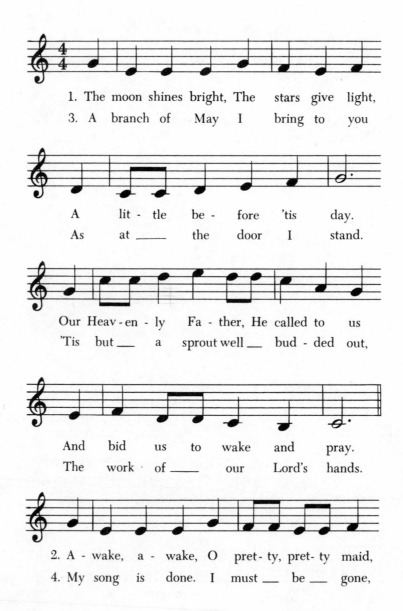

1. The moon shines bright, The stars give light,
3. A branch of May I bring to you

A lit - tle be - fore 'tis day.
As at ___ the door I stand.

Our Heav - en - ly Fa - ther, He called to us
'Tis but ___ a sprout well ___ bud - ded out,

And bid us to wake and pray.
The work of ___ our Lord's hands.

2. A - wake, a - wake, O pret - ty, pret - ty maid,
4. My song is done. I must ___ be ___ gone,

164

Out   of   your   drow - sy   dream.
No   long - er   can   I   stay.

And   step in - to   your dair - y   be - low
God   bless you   all,   both great ___   and small,

And   fetch   me   a   bowl   of   cream.
And   send   you   a   joy - ful   May.

Descant for bells, flute, or voice

Sing "Ah" throughout.

MAKING MUSIC YOUR OWN

1. Sing the melody of "Kookaburra" to yourself. It has three phrases. Which phrase starts on the fifth step of the scale? Which phrase starts on the third step of the scale?

2. Which of these intervals is a fifth? a third? an octave?

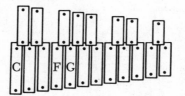

3. The picture of the tuned bells will help you answer questions about playing major scales.

When the tonal center is F, why do you have to play B♭?

When the tonal center is G, why do you have to play F♯?

When the tonal center is C, why is it unnecessary to play a sharp or a flat?

4. Name the tunes.

Tonal center: first space

Tonal center: second line

1. Can you hear how the sound of each of three chords (C, F, and G_7) is related to the others? Sing as you listen to the chord pattern of "Click Go the Shears." The first chord you will hear is the C chord. Stand still when you hear the C chord. Turn in place when you hear the F chord. Move forward when you hear the G_7 chord. If you miss, you must sit down.

INSTRUMENTAL MUSIC

1. Name each instrument shown below.

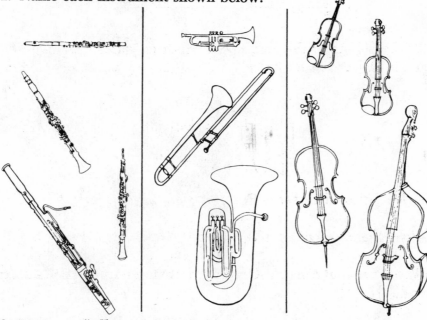

2. Listen to "Allegretto" by Rossini and identify each woodwind instrument as you hear it.

You have listened to music that describes a scene or tells a story and music that does not. You have also heard pieces from different kinds of suites. All of this music was composed in a certain design or form. You have studied these forms:

ABAB   ABA   Theme and variations

Listen to a composition you know and tell what its form is.

Listening to the composer

NORMAN DELLO JOIO

The Norman Dello Joio family gathers almost every evening for a family meeting. Often the three children play the piano for their parents. Sometimes Mr. Dello Joio improvises at the piano while Mrs. Dello Joio and Victoria make up dances. Some music Mr. Dello Joio improvised one evening led him to compose a book of piano duets especially for his children. Because each duet is based on some daily happening in his home, Mr. Dello Joio called the book *Family Album*.

Mr. Dello Joio and Justin watch and listen as Victoria and Norman, Jr., take their turn at the keyboard.

Mr. Dello Joio spends a great deal of time in his study. This is where he writes music for piano, voice, orchestra, chorus, and chamber groups.

169

Juliette

English Words by Margaret Marks   French Folk Song

To dance a polka, first practice the fundamental movement. Take sliding steps in time to the music, starting with your right foot leading. Then take sliding steps, starting with your left foot leading. When you can change from one foot leading to the other foot leading, without stopping in between, you are doing the polka step pattern.

You will discover that a hop will help you to change from one foot leading to the other foot leading. The hop is done quickly, and this makes the rhythm pattern uneven. Find the symbol for the hop in the polka rhythm.

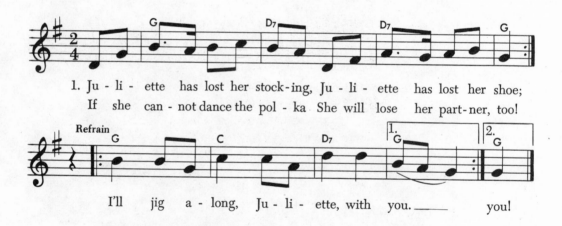

1. Ju - li - ette has lost her stock-ing, Ju - li - ette has lost her shoe;
   If she can - not dance the pol - ka She will lose her part-ner, too!

Refrain
I'll jig a - long, Ju - li - ette, with you. _____ you!

2. Juliette has lost her apron
   And her silken sash of blue.
   If she cannot dance the polka
   She will lose her partner, too!

3. Juliette has lost her bonnet
   And her frilly lace *fichu*....

4. Juliette has lost her hanky
   And her gloves so white and new....

170

Weggis Song

Swiss Folk Song

You can do a dance using the schottische step with this song.
Practice the step pattern first.

Rhythm pattern $\frac{4}{4}$

Step pattern   L   R   L   Hop   R   L   R   Hop

1. From Lu-cerne to_ Weg-gis on,
2. On the lake we_ all shall row, Hol- di-ri-di- a, hol- di-ri- a,
3. Weg- gis hills are_ not so far,

Shoes or stock- ings_ we won't don,
Look- ing at the _ fish be - low, Hol- di ri-di- a, hol- di- a.
We will all shout_"Hei - sa - sa,"

Refrain

Hol - di - ri - di - a, hol- di-ri-di - a, hol - di - ri - a,

Hol - di - ri - di - a, hol- di - ri-di - a, hol - di - a.

La Brandolina

English Words by Margaret Marks   Italian Folk Song

This song has two different sections. Can you hear which one is repeated and name the form of the song?

1. She'll   be   wed,   *la Bran - do - li - na,*
2. She's   a   bride,   *la Bran - do - li - na,*

To   the   groom who's nev - er   seen   her,
There's   a   ring   up - on   her   fin - ger,

La   bel - la   Bran - da,   la Vi - o - li - na,

La   bel - la   Bran - da,   la Vi - o - là!

Boys Now   she's   walk - ing   up   the   aisle
Girls Now   she's   mar - ried   to   her   spouse,

Hid - ing a tear or hid - ing a smile?
How will he take her in - to his house?

Will she swear to love and o - bey?
O - pen up the door, ___ of course!

Will she leave by run - ning a - way?
Pick her up and take her a - cross!

La bel - la Bran - da, la Vi - o - li - na,

La bel - la Bran - da, la Vi - o - là!

Play this pattern on a tambourine to accompany section A. Notice that the pattern starts on an upbeat, as the song does.

In section B, play the rhythm of the melody on a tambourine.

Don Gato

English Words by Margaret Marks   Mexican Folk Song

This is a story told in song. It is called a *ballad*. Take turns
singing a verse of the story.

1. Oh, Se - ñor   Don Ga - to   was   a   cat,_____
2. "I   a - dore   you!" wrote   the   la - dy   cat,_____

On   a   high,   red   roof   Don Ga - to   sat._____
Who was   fluff - y,   white,   and   nice and   fat._____

He   went there   to   read   a   let - ter,
There was   not   a   sweet - er   kit - ty,   meow, meow, meow,

Where the   read - ing   light was   bet - ter,
In   the   coun - try   or   the   cit - y,   meow, meow, meow,

'Twas   a   love   note   for   Don   Ga - to!_____
And she   said   she'd   wed   Don   Ga - to!_____

174

3. Oh, Don Gato jumped so happily
   He fell off the roof and broke his knee,
   Broke his ribs and all his whiskers, meow, meow, meow,
   And his little solar plexus, meow, meow, meow,
   "*¡Ay, carramba!*" cried Don Gato!

4. Then the doctors all came on the run
   Just to see if something could be done,
   And they held a consultation, meow, meow, meow,
   About how to save their patient, meow, meow, meow,
   How to save Señor Don Gato!

5. But in spite of everything they tried
   Poor Señor Don Gato up and died,
   Oh, it wasn't very merry, meow, meow, meow,
   Going to the cemetery, meow, meow, meow,
   For the ending of Don Gato!

6. When the funeral passed the market square
   Such a smell of fish was in the air
   Though his burial was slated, meow, meow, meow,
   He became re-animated! meow, meow, meow,
   He came back to life, Don Gato!

L'apprenti pastoureau (The Careless Shepherd)

English Version by Margaret Marks   French Folk Song

Discover the tune from the notation:

1. How many phrases are there in the song? Are any of them alike?

2. Study the meter sign. How many steady beats are there in a measure?

3. Study the rhythm of the melody. Does the song begin on a strong beat, or an upbeat? Tap the rhythm of the melody.

4. The tune starts on the tonal center. What is the highest note? What is the lowest note? Follow the notes on the staff and sing the tune while listening to the autoharp chords.

1. Quand j'é - tais   chez mon   pè - re,   ap - pren - ti   pas - tou - reau,
1. When   I   lived   with   my   fa - ther, to __   pay   for   my   keep,

Il   m'a   mis   dans   la   lan - de   pour gar - der   les   trou - peaux.
I   was   sent   to   the   pas - tures and __   told   to   herd   sheep.

Refrain

Trou - peaux,   trou - peaux,   je   n'en __   a - vais   guè - re,
Poor   sheep,   poor sheep!   I   had __   hard - ly   an - y,

Trou - peaux,   trou - peaux,   je   n'en __   a - vais   beaux.
Poor   sheep,   poor   sheep,   I   had __   hard - ly   one.

176

2. Mais je n'en avais guère,
   Je n'avais qu'trois agneaux
   Et le loup de la plaine
   M'a mangé le plus beau.

2. *No, I had hardly any,*
   Just three I possessed;
   And the wolf from the prairie
   Caught the one I liked best.

3. Pour fair' danser le village
   Dessous le grand ormeau
   Et les jeun's et les vieilles,
   Les pieds dans les sabots.

3. *Now they dance in the village*
   And I pipe for my keep;
   Farewell to the pasture,
   Farewell to the sheep!

Listening to the autoharp chords will help you to sing either part in the refrain. The lower part follows the melodic contour, but a third lower.

Practice playing this tune on the soprano recorder. Find a partner so that you can play the refrain in two parts.

Make New Friends

Round

Make new friends, but keep the old,

One is sil - ver and the oth - er gold.

177

Early One Morning

English Folk Song

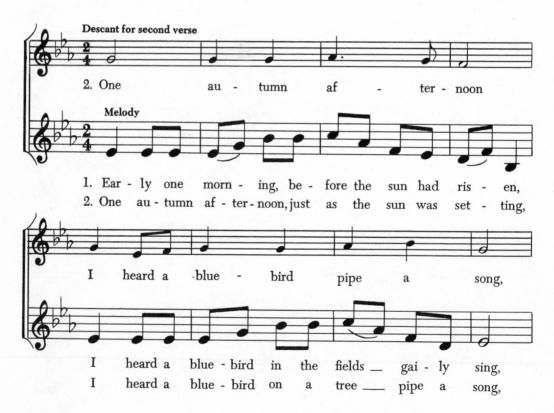

Descant for second verse

2. One au - tumn af - ter - noon

Melody

1. Ear - ly one morn - ing, be - fore the sun had ris - en,
2. One au - tumn af - ter - noon, just as the sun was set - ting,

I heard a blue - bird pipe a song,

I heard a blue - bird in the fields __ gai - ly sing,
I heard a blue - bird on a tree __ pipe a song,

178

"Fare - well! Cold winds blow;

"South winds are blow - ing, Green grass is grow - ing,
"Fare - well! We're go - ing, Cold winds are blow - ing,

We'll be back when the days grow long."

We __ come to her - ald the mer - ry __ spring."
But __ we'll be back __ when the days __ grow __ long."

Cindy

Southern Banjo Tune

1. I wish I was an ap - ple, A - hang - in' on a tree;
2. She took me to her par - lor, She cooled me with her fan,

And ev - 'ry time my Cin - dy passed She'd take a bite of me.
She swore I was the pur - tiest thing in the shape of mor - tal man.

You ought to see my Cin - dy, She lives a - way down South;
I wish I had a nee - dle, As fine as I could sew,

She is so sweet the hon - ey bees All swarm a - round her mouth.
I'd sew that gal to my coat - tail, And down the road I'd go.

Refrain

Get a - long home, _____ Get a - long home, _____

Melody

Get a - long home, Cin - dy, Cin - dy, Get a - long home, Cin - dy, Cin - dy,

180

Get a - long home, _____ I'll mar - ry you some day.

Get a - long home, Cin - dy, Cin - dy, I'll mar - ry you some day.

The Hole in the Bucket

American Folk Song

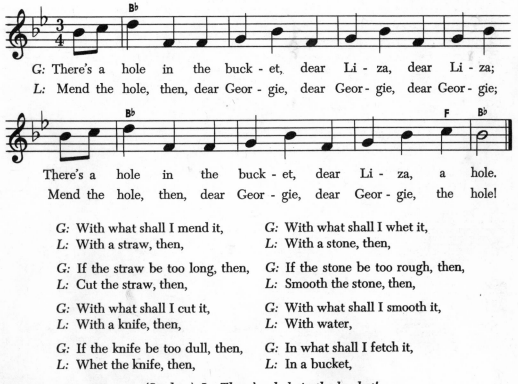

G: There's a hole in the buck - et, dear Li - za, dear Li - za;
L: Mend the hole, then, dear Geor - gie, dear Geor - gie, dear Geor - gie;

There's a hole in the buck - et, dear Li - za, a hole.
Mend the hole, then, dear Geor - gie, dear Geor - gie, the hole!

G: With what shall I mend it,
L: With a straw, then,

G: If the straw be too long, then,
L: Cut the straw, then,

G: With what shall I cut it,
L: With a knife, then,

G: If the knife be too dull, then,
L: Whet the knife, then,

G: With what shall I whet it,
L: With a stone, then,

G: If the stone be too rough, then,
L: Smooth the stone, then,

G: With what shall I smooth it,
L: With water,

G: In what shall I fetch it,
L: In a bucket,

(Spoken) L: There's a hole in the bucket!

Don't Stay Away

Spiritual

One part of this song is to be sung as a "call and response." Take turns singing the solo part.

All

My Lord says there's room e - nough, —

Room e - nough in the heav - en for us all.

My Lord says there's room e - nough, — So don't — stay a - way.

Solo

Oh, broth- er,   Oh, broth- er,
Oh, sis - ter,   Oh, sis - ter,

Chorus

Don't stay a - way, —   Don't stay a - way, —

All

Oh, broth- er,   Don't stay a - way, —   Don't — stay a - way.
Oh, sis - ter,

182

Die Musici (Music Alone Shall Live)

Old German Round

I

Him - mel und Er - de müs - sen ver - gehn;
All things shall per - ish from un - der the sky;

II

A - ber die Mu - si - ci, a - ber die Mu - si - ci,
Mu - sic a - lone shall live, mu - sic a - lone shall live,

A - ber die Mu - si - ci blei - ben be - stehn.
Mu - sic a - lone shall live, nev - er to die.

Which of these would you like to perform for an end-of-school program?

THE SEAS AROUND US

Other Children (poem)
Atlantic Ocean
Mediterranean Sea
Caribbean Sea
North Sea
Pacific Ocean

SING AND DANCE AROUND
THE WORLD

American Square Dance
African Dances
East Mediterranean Dance
Russian Dance
English Country Dance
Hawaiian Stick Dance

Japanese Dance
European Waltz
European Schottische
European Polka

MAKING MUSIC YOUR OWN

The Piper (poem)
San Sereni
Raisins and Almonds
Cretan Dance
¡Qué bueno es saber tocar!
Mañana
The Judge's Ball
Click Go the Shears
Sakura
Rarakatom!
L'apprenti pastoureau

Index

INTEGRATED LISTENING SELECTIONS

POEMS

STORIES

OTHER INTEGRATED ACTIVITIES